A Lacanian Theory of Curriculum in Higher Education

Fernando M. Murillo

A Lacanian Theory of Curriculum in Higher Education

The Unfinished Symptom

Fernando M. Murillo
University of British Columbia
Vancouver, BC, Canada

ISBN 978-3-319-99764-3   ISBN 978-3-319-99765-0 (eBook)
https://doi.org/10.1007/978-3-319-99765-0

Library of Congress Control Number: 2018954557

© The Editor(s) (if applicable) and The Author(s) 2018
This work is subject to copyright. All rights are solely and exclusively licensed by the Publisher, whether the whole or part of the material is concerned, specifically the rights of translation, reprinting, reuse of illustrations, recitation, broadcasting, reproduction on microfilms or in any other physical way, and transmission or information storage and retrieval, electronic adaptation, computer software, or by similar or dissimilar methodology now known or hereafter developed.
The use of general descriptive names, registered names, trademarks, service marks, etc. in this publication does not imply, even in the absence of a specific statement, that such names are exempt from the relevant protective laws and regulations and therefore free for general use.
The publisher, the authors and the editors are safe to assume that the advice and information in this book are believed to be true and accurate at the date of publication. Neither the publisher nor the authors or the editors give a warranty, express or implied, with respect to the material contained herein or for any errors or omissions that may have been made. The publisher remains neutral with regard to jurisdictional claims in published maps and institutional affiliations.

Cover illustration: © Melisa Hasan

This Palgrave Pivot imprint is published by the registered company Springer Nature Switzerland AG
The registered company address is: Gewerbestrasse 11, 6330 Cham, Switzerland

Foreword

Every thought, conceived in the flame of intuition, born in the pain of thinking, constitutes a new clearing. Where we find a cluttered or clogged situation, where we find a knotted and tangled mess, where disorder and chaos have choked all life and breathe, there we find a dead and thoughtless place. These moribund places abound in our present age in a way that is not unprecedented in kind, but is surely unique in scale. The sheer scope of the catastrophe is catastrophic.

At the turn of the twentieth century, a group of modern shipbuilders using the tools of Romanticism, Existentialism, Phenomenology, Pragmatism, and Psychoanalysis built the first vessels that would sail into what would become modernity's most violent and absurd chapter. As the saying goes, history's repetitions come first as tragedy and second as farce. We have seen this saying play out from then to now, a century removed from the first great war. In that sequence, certain aspects stand out. Perhaps no institution has been less aware of this epochal situation—and of its own role in its absurdity—than the modern compulsory school. Surely no academic field has been so heartless and unmoved as the one we call "Education." Despite the constant refrains of reform, today's common sense about schooling, education, curriculum, and teaching are not such much reformed as they are *deformed*.

As with all rules, there are the exceptions. In the late 1960s and early 1970s, Paul Khlor, a professor of curriculum at Ohio State University, shared a vision of curriculum inspired by his own genius, tested upon his many years working as a school principal. His vision was not realized through his pen, but through his teaching. In his student William Pinar's vocabulary, it was Khlor's "subjective presence" that communicated this irreducible vision of curriculum. As with all the great teachers who do not write (e.g. Socrates and Jesus), Khlor's ideas were passed down to and through students like Timothy Leonard, the aforementioned Pinar, and Pinar's student, Janet Miller. These ideas came together within a community of scholars who founded the field we now call "curriculum theory" or "curriculum studies", a movement that initiated a full reconceptualization of curriculum. The Reconceptualists used Khlor's vision, articulated and developed most boldly by Pinar, as their fuel. The Reconceptualists took up this work within the legacy and traditions of those shipbuilders of the humanities at the turn of the century, after their vessels barely survived the two great wars. They sought to awaken the field of Education out of its social scientific slumber and point to a vision of curriculum that was not limited by the near sightedness of the institutional school.

Today, what little remains of the Reconceptualist tradition in curriculum has in many ways forgotten and abandoned these projects. Sadly, this tradition never became truly apostolic. But, again, there are the exceptions that prove the rule. Here, in this book, we have the work of a student of a student of Paul Khlor, a student of William Pinar, Fernando Murillo, his first book in English. When one reads Murillo's proposal in this book, it must be read within this genealogical and historical context. Murillo himself affirms this exegetical key. When he writes "I propose an approach to psychoanalytic critique organized in a guiding grid of thought that brings together elements from psychoanalytic as well as curricular theory", he is proposing more than a simple study (something important in its own right). He is moving towards an epochal reorganization.

In this short book, Murillo gestures to something radical and ambitious: a *ressourcement*, a return to the sources of the modern humanities and the reconceptualists of curriculum. He writes, movingly, that "Ignoring the psychoanalytic constitution of subjectivity in its core dimensions of desire, libidinal ties, suffering, and anxiety cannot go without consequences in the formative enterprise of curriculum work". While Murillo clearly speaks at the classic confessional interval of interiority, I also hear him modulate into a register that critiques the present and profound ignorance of the field of Education, including the state of the study of curriculum. This is not a purely critical move and Murillo is careful to absolutely distinguish his ideas from the "critical" traditions, above all critical pedagogy. What we find instead is a brilliantly destructive act of fidelity, faithful to the modern tradition of psychoanalysis in its widest sense and the project of the reconceptualization of curriculum in its original spirit.

Murillo avoids fad and group-think cliches in his bold embrace of the difficult humanism that "is not to make us feel better, or 'produce' or ameliorate anything, but to allow us to be ourselves more authentically". This authenticity results in nothing more or less than the ability—indeed, the courage—to look at the full scope of the catastrophe, inside and out. The reader who is not called to an existential conversion in these pages is in most need of its conviction. For my part, I see and hear it as a proposal that tests the very possibility of a future for curriculum and, indeed, Education as an academic discipline. Rather than challenge through novelty, however, Murillo goes back into the idea of *Bildung* and brings it forward into a powerful series of associations.

With respect to his method, Murillo embraces the classic descriptive scope of psychoanalysis and phenomenology while at the same time turning it psychically against the technocratic clutter of the common sense notion of educational "practice." He insists that:

> This expectation and demand for theory to 'do' things is, as we have shown, a symptomatic expression of a certain anxiety about being in the world. A world that is experienced as frightening in its complexity and unpredictability, that might expose our fragility, and that opens up the possibility of having to face the unknown existential aspects of our human condition, is met with a compulsion to act, to intervene, to prescribe how things should be done rather than describe them as they are.

It is in this aspect of method where I find Murillo at his most original and virtuosic. He takes up the psychoanalytic tradition on its own uncompromising terms of specificity, yet he avoids the pitfalls of "application" by navigating its terrain philosophically, across practical and phenomenological sites of inquiry. At the same time, he freely associates the psychoanalytic tradition to curriculum in the reconceptualist tradition—and the wider *Bildung* tradition of education and the existing work on the matter—without stepping outside the central domain of the subject and the person. The result of his efforts is not so much a "result" as they are an *inspiration*, a hope in a time of increasing hopelessness.

In his final line—which I will not spoil by quoting for the reader here—Murillo brings us to the spectacular site of love as the clearing that his symptomatic theory of curriculum unties. *The Unfinished Symptom* is a clearing, then, in the most fundamental sense of transcendental clarity: the clearing that destroys what is destructible to reveal what is eternal. In these pages, gentle reader, you will find an unbinding of life and breathe from the clutches of death. Let it burn and hurt.

Vancouver, BC, Canada   Samuel D. Rocha
March 2018

Contents

1 Introduction   1

2 The Formation of the Subject: Curriculum as an Unfinished Symptom   9

3 Critique: Between Theory and Method   33

4 Analyzing Symptoms in Policy: A Psychoanalytic Reading   61

5 Concluding Thoughts   83

Index   89

CHAPTER 1

Introduction

Abstract Two aspects of educational experience speak of the affinity between curricular and psychoanalytic inquiry: one is that it is an act fundamentally mediated by the question for the formation of a self into a subject. The other is that the educational process of cultivation of subjectivity is one that is marked by symptomatic expression. What establishes a link between Lacanian psychoanalysis and the field of curriculum studies appears initially as a concern for the existential drama of being and becoming, the universal and substantial aspects of humanity that operate behind the practical operations of education, and the attention to desire, suffering, and enjoyment that inscribe our biographies. This introduction delineates a more specific account of the pertinence of Lacanian psychoanalysis for the understanding of curriculum.

Keywords Lacanian psychoanalysis · Curriculum · Educational experience · Subjectivity

In 1937, Sigmund Freud famously declared education to be an impossible profession. Educating—just like analyzing and governing—Freud remarked, is an occupation "in which one can be sure beforehand of achieving unsatisfying results". The constant risk of failure in these professions, we learn from Freud, is predicated on their highly contextual nature, their permanent standing at the threshold between the terminable and the interminable, and perhaps most importantly, on account of the multivariate ways we symptomatize the antagonism between the principles of reality and pleasure.

Around four decades later, and during a press conference in Rome, Jacques Lacan—known for revitalizing psychoanalysis through his work marked by a radical "return to Freud"—brought back the statement Freud had made about the impossible professions. Focusing on education, and educators, in particular, Lacan indicated that "there is no shortage of people who receive the stamp of approval [and who are thus] authorized to educate". "This does not mean", he continued, "that they have the slightest idea what is involved in educating. People don't perceive very clearly what they are wanting to do when they educate". Then, and in highlighting the appearance of symptoms in the act of educating, he adds that educators "become gripped with anxiety when they think about what it is to educate (…) One perceives…that at the root of education there lies a certain idea of what one must do to create men - as if it were education that did so" (2008, pp. 55–56). What might this tell us about the relationship between psychoanalysis and education?

The difficulty in knowing exactly what it is that takes place in the act of educating, the anxiety inherent to educating and being educated, and the deeply felt intuition that it is a process related to the creation of men (and potentially also their destruction) are aspects that illuminate two interrelated dimensions of education. One is that it is an act fundamentally mediated by the question for the formation of a self into a subject. The other is that this process of cultivation of subjectivity is one that is marked by symptomatic expression.

What establishes a link, then, between Lacanian psychoanalysis and the field of curriculum studies appears initially as a concern for the existential drama of being and becoming, the universal and substantial aspects of humanity that operate behind the practical operations of education, and the attention to desire, suffering, and enjoyment that inscribe our biographies. Importantly for this perspective is that these aspects just mentioned find expression, as well as concealment, through the signifying chains of words and symptoms.

But pursuing the challenge of delineating an understanding of the phenomenon of curriculum from a specifically Lacanian psychoanalytic perspective requires that we situate first the notion of curriculum we are working from, the tradition in which it stands, and that we sketch out the specificity of a psychoanalytic approach based on the work of Jacques Lacan.

Historically, the academic field of curriculum has been dominated—at least in the Anglo-American context—by a view that treats curriculum as a technical matter of designing, developing, implementing, and evaluating predefined outcomes in a school setting. A practice informed to a large extent by cognitive-behavioristic psychology, positivistic sociology, economics, and other disciplines inclined to social engineering, curriculum came to be seen as a matter of schooling, disciplinary content, teaching and learning, and techniques to make these processes of transmission and absorption more effective. In our times, such effectiveness is measured in relation to the achievement of higher test scores. This is what we can refer to as a traditional approach to curriculum.

However, and in contrast to this approach characterized by its reliance on predefined behavioral objectives, a radical shift started to take place among some scholars in the field of curriculum studies in the 1970s, a shift that came to be known as the Reconceptualization of curriculum. The reconceptualization represents a challenge to the established tradition, shifting the focus of attention from the managerial aspects of schooling and instruction, to an intellectual and scholarly understanding of educational experience (Pinar, 1999). The experience of educating and being educated is studied primarily in its cultural, psychic, gendered, philosophical, and historical dimensions.

Subjective reconstruction, not politics or instructional tricks, is what we find at the heart of a reconceptualized field of curriculum studies.

In its interest for the subjectively existing individual, and the potentiality for subjective reconstruction, a reconceptualized perspective of curriculum shows affinity with a notion of education that, in the German tradition, came to be expressed in the term *Bildung*. Loosely understood as the "cultivation of the inner self", it is an understanding of education as a self-initiated process of formation directed at the enrichment of sensibility and character. In this sense, the expansion of our human substance (the ultimate task of existence in this view) is something that occurs through the practice of study: a spiritually enhancing discipline of intellectual engagement with alterity and knowledge. Important for this tradition, as Wilhelm von Humboldt—the first in developing an academic theory of *Bildung*—insisted, the necessary foundation for an authentic education is to be found in the humanities: literature, philosophy, art, history, linguistics, and religion.

These elements that conform a notion of curriculum in a reconceptualized perspective are what constitute the concept of curriculum used and affirmed throughout this book.

Interestingly, and when it comes to the formation of a psychoanalyst, both Sigmund Freud and Jacques Lacan maintained that those in the process of becoming analysts must first become well versed in the humanities, just as *Bildung* and a reconceptualized understanding of curriculum emphasize. But what makes a Lacanian approach to psychoanalysis distinct? While the work of Jacques Lacan cannot be understood but in direct relation to Freud,[1] there are some emphases in Lacan that cast psychoanalytic work in a different light.

Suffice it to briefly mention at this point three of these aspects that help clarify the specificity of psychoanalysis in Lacanian terms.

The first one refers to the frames of reference to understand and talk about psychic phenomena. Before Lacan, the study and practice of psychoanalysis had remained largely confined to the dimension of the clinical, and it struggled to make sense of its findings with a vocabulary and mindset that was still heavily influenced by biological determinations. Although Freud had opened new ground and demonstrated outstanding insights through the use of analogy with Greek mythopoiesis, Lacan brought to psychoanalysis an approach more firmly rooted in philosophy, thus providing a wider frame of reference and a language that better captured the existential dimensions of psychic phenomena. Lacan's study of Hegel and Heidegger, for example, proved to be essential to the development of his approach to selfhood.

The second aspect refers to the dimension of language. Perhaps one of the best-known insights from Lacan is that "the unconscious is structured like a language". This apparently simple phrase contains within it a myriad of complex implications. It also points to the fact that Lacan took words seriously. One of the first implications is that the "signifier"—Lacan's preferred term to refer to words—takes center place of attention, as it is what anchors the otherwise endless sliding of "signifieds" or meanings. In this way, Lacan subverts the classic linguistic model of Ferdinand de Saussure,[2] giving precedence to the signifier (words) over and above the signified (meaning). This inversion takes us to another

---

[1] At the end of his life, Lacan made his allegiance to Freud even clearer: "it is up to you to be Lacanian if you wish: I am a Freudian".

[2] For Saussure, a sign is composed of a unity between a signified and a signifier i.e. a mental concept and its corresponding sound-image. These two components are, in his view, inseparable just as the two sides of a sheet of paper. To illustrate this relation, Saussure used a diagram where the Signified is placed above the Signifier.

implication. Since the unconscious is structured like a language, the unconscious material (such as drives and desire) find expression through signifiers, using words as a vehicle. Symptoms—the expression of conflicts of desire—can then be interpreted from their articulation in language. As Lacan made clear, "a signifier has meaning only through its relation to another signifier. The truth of symptoms resides in this articulation" (Écrits, 2006, p. 195).

The third aspect, which is closely related to the previous one, is the erasure of the distinction between normal and abnormal. While this distinction was still prevalent in Freud, for Lacan, symptoms are existential expressions that are constitutive of the subject. Analytic work, then, is not about "fixing" the appearance of symptoms but about recognizing their origin and direction. After all, that is precisely what the symptom wants: to bring attention and acknowledgment. "The subject's personality", Lacan points out, "is structured like a symptom that his personality feels to be foreign;… like a symptom, his personality harbours a meaning, that of a repressed conflict" (Écrits, 2006, p. 283).

These three aspects that make up a distinctively Lacanian approach to psychoanalysis speak of the pertinence and potential explanatory power of this approach to read and understand situations in the larger context of culture and politics, and not just what happens in psychotherapy.

An interest in the psychic workings that explain individual and social life expressed through psychoanalytic discourse is, of course, not new in educational work. In recent years, there seems to be a revival of interest in psychoanalysis, which is expressed in the growing number of authors claiming to work from such perspective in their analyses of situations of teaching and learning. However, and as Lacan had already warned, in spite of the growing prevalence in use of terms derived from psychoanalytic experience, much of the work being done in academic circles under its name, represents, in fact, a departure from the doctrine of psychoanalysis as authentically set by Freud. A psychoanalysis that concerns itself mainly with a theory of the ego, and with the intent of strengthening that ego, is for Lacan not only a "lack of theoretical sophistication" but "an enormous error". In his return to Freud, what distinguishes psychoanalytic technique is, for Lacan, a concern for "the subject's relation to the signifier" (Écrits, 2006, p. 395).

We hear an echo of a similar warning in the Austrian educator and psychoanalyst Siegfried Bernfeld who, in criticizing the social-scientific inflection of a psychology that is blind to desire and the drives, refers to such scholars of education as "astronomers who sleep at night and by day let others tell them of the stars" (1973, p. 20).

In much of the literature today that brings together education and psychoanalysis we find the same problems that Bernfeld saw in his time: an almost exclusive focus on pair groups (parent–child, teacher–student, and the assumption of education as an organized and quasi-homogeneous collection of pair groups), a disregard for the internal world of the subjectively existing individual, and a feeble theoretical foundation for the claims being done. Bernfeld takes a bolder step when he declares that "only when this kind of psychology [the 'superficial' investigation of perception, association, and thinking] is replaced by the teaching of Freud, who puts development, drives, and character into the center of concern, can the science of education be provided with a foundation" (p. 46).

And yet, even among much of the psychoanalytic discourse in education today, we continue to find a focus on aspects of schooling, teacher–student relation, learning, and teaching. We also find a strong accent on social–emotional relations, learning, and professional development, along with other forms of strengthening the ego.

One of the problems with these approaches is that, by focusing exclusively on consciousness, agency, acts and events, they lose sight of other aspects that Lacan chose to emphasize precisely because they stand at the root of the former ones, namely, *jouissance* (enjoyment and suffering which cannot be properly symbolized), symbolic identification (which runs against enjoyment, and yet decisive in the formation of the I), the function of the signifier, and their appearance in symptomatic formations.

The problem with focusing almost exclusively on issues like experience, cognition, ego psychology, ideology, practices, or mere historical accounts, is that a series of conditions, which are presupposed, are taken for granted. But not in Lacanv. In what can be read as a phenomenology of the ego, he addresses the "I" at the center of our dealings with ourselves and with the world, delving not only into the more detailed psychic dynamics, but their more existential character.

Hence, a Lacanian approach is particularly productive in the analysis and critique of curriculum for at least two reasons:

On the one hand, and from its philosophical inflection, it allows for a broader reading of the process of formation, outside the restrains and particularities of schooling. The Lacanian analytical categories of the Symbolic, Imaginary, and the Real (the topography through which Lacan understands the configuration of subjectivity) are lenses to read a variety of cultural expressions, as they appear and develop in our specific contexts, in our day-to-day engagement in and with the world. Put differently, to think with Lacan may allow us to get "under the hood" of educational and lived experience, and into the subtler and yet decisive dynamics that explain their phenomena, that find their roots in the universality of the human drama.

On the other hand, and as we mentioned earlier, the distinction between normal and abnormal (or pathological) disappears. Though a cause of suffering, symptoms are no longer a pathology to be treated or a malaise that requires fixing within the context of the clinic but are rather constitutive expressions of the self that can be read, recognized, and dealt with in the wider cultural context. Symptoms are signifiers that signal aspects of our present configuration of personality and leave traces of the direction and trajectory of our desires. Hinging on enjoyment, some symptoms tend to persist. Paying attention to the nature and structure of the symptom can allow for a productive reading of cultural, sexual, sociopolitical and, of course, educational expressions of subjectivity.

Working with and through educational issues from a Lacanian form of psychoanalysis requires both knowing *about* Lacan—through secondary sources—but also *of* and *from* Lacan himself—through careful and systematic study of his works. Through such a practice one finds that a psychoanalytic understanding in Lacanian terms necessarily involves a return to Freud: an analytical stance that digs behind what shows itself as apparent, a capacity to read and interpret the accidents of human existence through their mythopoetic substance, and a rejection of any form of approach to analytical work directed at merely strengthening the ego.

What we learn from Lacan in the field of curriculum studies is not only an attentiveness to the word, the signifier, to language and the ways in which it covers, displaces, but also brings to the surface expressions of desire. We also learn to develop an openness to grapple with the ongoing, open-ended, and fundamentally noncoincidental nature of our process of becoming, the both tragic and sublime pull and push of an ego, an ideal-ego, and an ego-ideal: the substance of curricular work at its purest. In other words, the struggle of the relation between who I believe to be, who I believe I should be, and who I believe the Other wants me to be, a struggle that begins the moment we step into language and ends at death.

But perhaps most fundamentally, in working through a psychoanalytic approach as we see it modeled by Lacan, we find that this work invites a particular attitude toward the phenomena that brings our attention. It is an attitude of incisive questioning and critique informed by academic knowledge and a compassionate, gentle attentiveness to the drama, the sufferings, joys, and transformations that may occur when we confront (or are confronted) by the real.

In the end, it is love—as Lacan made sure to reminds us—what unties and severs the knots of the symptomatic expressions of our coming-to-be-in-the-world.

With this theoretical impetus as a background, in this book, I set out to accomplish the following three tasks:

1. To propose a theorization of curriculum in Lacanian psychoanalytic terms, bringing to attention its symptomatic dimension.
2. To follow the elements that the theorization of curriculum as symptom provide to their implications for a method of critique.
3. To demonstrate the method as a form of research, applying it to the analysis of the text of a current international curricular policy.

References

Bernfeld, S. (1973). *Sisyphus or the Limits of Education*. Berkeley: University of California Press.

Lacan, J. (2006). *Écrits*. New York: W. W. Norton.

Lacan, J. (2008). *My Teaching*. London: Verso.

Pinar, W. (1999). The Reconceptualization of Curriculum Studies. *Counterpoints, 70*. Contemporary Curriculum Discourses: Twenty Years of JCT (pp. 483–497).

CHAPTER 2

The Formation of the Subject: Curriculum as an Unfinished Symptom

Abstract This chapter explores the relation between curriculum and the formation of subjectivity, i.e. the notion of "who we are" as individuals. This relation is theorized by positing as a main premise that the curricular act is decisively involved in the structuration of the subject by means of the psychoanalytic phenomenon of the transference. A crucial insight that emerges from this theorization is the understanding that curriculum functions as an unfinished symptom. The chapter closes with a discussion of the notion of curriculum as a "conversation" from the psychoanalytic perspective of the transference involved in and through the dialogical encounter.

Keywords Curriculum · Subjectivity · Psychoanalysis · Symptom · Transference

INTRODUCTION

That curriculum is a situation that produces certain kinds of consequences other than that related exclusively to content learning or skills is a well-accepted notion. Especially among those of a more progressive and critical bend, there seems to be an agreement that through curricular activity we learn ways of being in the world; that we construct a vision of ourselves and those around us, mainly due to the fact that the pedagogical situation is imbued not only in technical content, but in political, social, and cultural beliefs that shape both students' and teachers' dispositions.

Today, in a climate of ever-growing homogeneity and standardization of educational practices, the question for the subjectively existing individual reoccurs, and perhaps with more urgency than before. At a time when more institutions of higher education are transitioning toward market models of education-and competency-based curricular organization,[1] it has become a challenge for them to differentiate what defines their institution in its singularity, what sets them apart from the project and identity of other institutions, and what "seal" they are imprinting on their graduates. But beyond issues of skill qualification, the more pressing question that remains is that of the formation of the subject as a human person. But for a traditional approach to curriculum this is not an issue of particular concern. Recall here that for Franklin Bobbitt (1913)—one of the fathers of modern curriculum theory and design, who introduced the notion that education required external standards—education is "a shaping process as much as the manufacture of steel rails" (p. 12). Along with equating education to a mechanical and objectifying process of manufacture, he places education in the realm of the natural and even biological, thus shrouding it in the appearance of inevitability and predetermination: "In the field of biological production, of which education constitutes one sort, the factor of growth enters in to complicate and in part to obscure the working of our principles", Bobbitt laments (p. 13). Within the same tradition, in 1949, Ralph Tyler contributed to further establish a notion of education seen primarily as an objective and controllable process of production, one that can be predicted by objectives and measured by testing.

Not surprisingly, the question for the cultivation of the human spirit had been effectively removed from educational discourse. But as we will see later on, disavowing does not mean getting rid of. As the reader will recall from the introduction, the shift that started taking place in the field of curriculum studies known as the reconceptualization was a response to the dehumanizing terms that the traditional approaches to curriculum had started to impose on education. Just like in the German

---

[1] In a trend fostered and directed by international economic organizations such as the World Bank and the OECD, universities all over Europe and in most countries in the American continent are adopting curricular designs based on practical skills, the use of quantitative standards of measurement, and imposing cost-efficiency rationales on their programs, causing a reduction in the length of degree programs, the reduction of classroom interaction on exchange for computer platforms, a lowering of standards for student admission and graduation, among other transformations to the spirit and purpose of the university.

notion of *Bildung*, a reconceptualized perspective conceives education primarily in terms of a process of being and becoming, a matter of expanding our human substance, in attention to intellect, body, emotion, and spirit. The realm of culture, not biology or economics, is what drives the process of cultivation of interiority.

Curriculum theorist Dwayne Huebner made important contributions to a reconceptualized understanding of curriculum by way of attentive study of philosophy, particularly through the work of thinkers such as José Ortega y Gasset and Martin Heidegger, who delved deeply into the question of being. In a piece from 1966 entitled "Curricular language and classrooms meanings", Huebner strongly criticized conventional classroom language, highlighting the need to focus again on the human subject and its complexity at the center of educational practice. He refers to the term "learning", for example, as a "tyrannical myth" that has taken deep roots in curricular language. As a term that has displaced the subject, he tells us:

> "Indeed, curricular language seems rather ludicrous when the complexity and the mystery of a fellow human being is encompassed in that technical term of control – the "learner". Think of it – there standing before the educator is a being partially hidden in the cloud of unknowing. For centuries the poet has sung of his near infinitudes; the theologian has preached of his depravity and hinted of his participation in the divine; the philosopher has struggled to encompass him in his systems, only to have him repeatedly escape; (…) and the man engaged in curriculum has the temerity to reduce this being to a single term – "learner"". (1999, pp. 102–103)

But it is not until 1976 when, partially inspired by Huebner's work, a young William Pinar marks a definitive shift in curricular studies in a move away from attention to schooling and toward subjectivity instead. During a conference on curriculum theory in Milwaukee—one attended by Ralph Tyler and Elliot Eisner—Pinar read what proved to be a controversial paper in response to both the traditional and the seemingly progressive approaches to curriculum. In what was considered an *avant-garde* theoretical position, he reframed the reconceptualist approach as one that rejected the "intellectual imperialism of the social sciences in the field of education" and felt "disdain for experiments and other contemporary forms of pseudo-empiricism". Further, he made a crucial distinction between education and schooling. "What is practiced in schools often bears little or no relation to the process that is education", he asserts, positing educational experience as the primary interest of a reconceptualized view of curriculum. Education, in contrast to schooling, is conceived as a broad concept, one that is mediated fundamentally by one's own biographic situation. As such, to talk about education means to talk about the "intellectual and psychosocial development of individuals", to pay attention to "body and feeling", to refer to the self-initiated discipline of study, and, overall, to the experience of subjective reconstruction and transformation.

With this paper, Pinar provoked a turning point in the field of curriculum studies, one that brought the focus of attention back to the subject at the center of educational experience and opened the way for a more careful and dedicated consideration of the problem of subjective reconstruction.

In the work of Jacques Lacan, the subject and its process of becoming is also a central focus of attention. This becomes apparent in one of his landmark works where he posits his theory of the "mirror stage". The full title of this paper from 1949 is a first indication of this interest: "The Mirror Stage as Formative of the Function of the I as Revealed in Psychoanalytic Experience".[2] In this paper, he explores the transformation that takes place in early infancy in terms of the transition from a "specular I" to a "social I". This transformation of a self into a subject is, as Lacan shows, a phenomenon of language, a change that takes place the moment we step into the realm of the symbolic. The notion of the subject as a "*parlêtre*"—a neologism introduced by Lacan to refer to the subject as a "speaking being"—further reaffirms his assertion that "the subject...is an effect of the signifier". It is language what sustains the phenomenon of the "transference"—the affective relation established between analyst and analysand, or between teacher and student—a relation composed of previous identifications with figures of authority, fantasies, expectations, affects, love, and hate. Later on, this chapter will further explore the notion of subjectivity from a Lacanian perspective and its implications for a theory of curriculum.

---

[2] The paper was to be delivered originally in 1936 but he was interrupted 10 minutes into his presentation and forced to step down, as the main organizer of the conference deemed it impenetrable. This did not discourage Lacan from continue to develop his theoretical (and stylistic) approach, and thirteen years later gave the same paper again, this time gaining international attention.

In exploring the relationship between curriculum and subject formation, the interest is not in confirming the already familiar notion that "something happens" to individuals in a pedagogical relationship, or that unconscious influences take place, but rather, the discussion is directed toward theorizing the modus operandi of such psychic influences in and through curricular work. The attempt is to complicate the way we think about curriculum from a Lacanian psychoanalytic perspective. By exploring the psychic dynamics involved and the performative work of language, I wish to posit as a main premise that the curricular act is decisively involved in the structuration of the subject by means of the psychoanalytic phenomenon of the transference. In addition, I want to suggest the claim that, by means of the transference, curriculum functions as an unfinished symptom. Throughout this chapter, I rely on the Freudian notion of the unconscious in general, and on the Lacanian notion of the transference in particular—by way of their contextualization in curricular theory in the work of Deborah Britzman and Peter Taubman—as a background to theorize the workings of curricular practice in psychic dynamics that affect the (re)construction of the subject *qua* individual.

CURRICULAR WORK AND ITS UNPREDICTABLE PSYCHIC CONSEQUENCES

...education does not just require crisis but is, in and of itself, an exemplary crisis... Deborah Britzman (2003b, p. 7)

to teach without hope, without focusing on outcomes, whether these are social revolution...or learning square roots...is to shift our attention to the palpably invisible...to the minor tremors, and the fleeting sensations that hover around or strike the corners of consciousness. Peter Taubman (2011, p. 186)

If we take curriculum as the ever-present question for "what knowledge is of most worth?", then clearly doing curriculum implies an act of selection. But an aspect that reconceptualists and post-critical theoreticians have helped to consider is that such act of selection constitutes at the same time and act of exclusion. Even though the process of doing curriculum is sometimes understood and presented as an objective and impartial selection of cultural contents (often by "experts" in each field), the question for what makes the excluded contents undesirable, or unimportant, reframe the process from the perspective of desire and its expression in the subjacent ideological and epistemological beliefs that guide that very process of inclusion/exclusion, determining what is important, valuable, and which discourses are given privilege over others in a certain context and time.

The power of deciding what and how other people are going to study (and not study), brings curriculum into the realm of ethical activity, not only because it decides and pre-stipulates the kind of experiences that others will have, but fundamentally because—in Foucauldian terms—that selection of knowledge, mediated and constituted by power relations has an impact in the configurations of identity of those involved in the pedagogical practice. In this context, it is interesting to note that for Tomás Tadeo Da Silva (2001) curriculum is often presented as a canon of universal culture, when in fact, it is a selection of a very particular type of culture: Eurocentric, white, masculine and heterosexual. As contents are not neutral, they are bound to have certain effects in the process of their manufacture, circulation, and consumption.

A similar concern seems to be shared by Eagleton, when he urges critics to be attentive to "the kinds of *effects* which discourses produce, and how they produce them" (cited in Bracher 1993, p. 3).

It is perhaps in the same logic and concern that Peter Grimmett calls for a reconceptualized curriculum design (2010). In his critical review of William Pinar's "Understanding Curriculum" (1995), Grimmett asserts that, "…the two aspects of curriculum understanding and curriculum creation must co-evolve if the power of re-conceptualist curriculum is to pervade the life-world of learning", and suggests that Pinar dismissed the issue of design, leaving for others to re-conceptualize the design of non-technicist curriculum, and by doing so, "ignored what institutional text does" (p. 242).

It is my assumption that Grimmett was perhaps trying to find ways to redress the cultural effects of the discursive practices of dominant groups, through a curriculum design that dealt explicitly with the cultural and political tenets of educational propositions. If the selection of knowledges and ways of thinking and being have an impact in the configuration of people's subjectivity and sense of agency, then it would make sense to try to come up with a design that would foster explicitly certain traits deemed as desirable in those involved in the pedagogical relation.

However, these designs might not actually produce the effects one would hope for.

This is clear in Anne Phelan's suspicion of designating prior identities via curriculum design, because "human beings constantly exceed and frustrate prior identifications, often contradicting their own expressed and deepest commitments", reason why "designating a prior identity... does not guarantee anything" (2010, p. 321).

In this tension between a liberatory call for action and the impossibility of teleological designs for identity formation, Grimmett draws an interesting point: institutional discourses do have an effect, as the scholarship of Critical Discourse Analysis has shown (see the work of Norman Fairclough, for example).

But are these effects predictable?

Phelan does not seem to think so, and she warns us again about the "incalculability of action", reminding us that "subjectivity is a quality of human interaction and not a set of characteristics individuals possess" (2010, p. 326). Jacques Lacan would agree. As he indicates in his *Écrits*, "every discourse derives its effects from the unconscious" (p. 701). Discourse then has effects, but since they are derived from the unconscious, they cannot be foreseen.

Phelan's view of subjectivity is in sync with psychoanalysis. As Deborah Britzman (2009) asserts, a defining trait of curricular work is that "all education suffers a radical fate of indeterminacy" (p. viii). I am not exactly sure that indeterminacy is what is "suffered". It certainly was not the case in older traditions of study. But the main point stands.

Even though pedagogical experience has shown the consistent failure at attempting to control outcomes via teleological curricular discourses, their existence and imposition should not be regarded as unproblematic. In Civilization and its Discontents (1957), Freud points out that inefficacious at realizing all their aims as some discourses can be, they never the less are not innocuous: they do produce effects. In view of the circumstances that the term "effect" can give the impression of referring to visible behaviors, or that they can be planned, controlled or traced back to a "cause", I prefer to turn to the language suggested by Britzman (2003b), when she refers to education as a process that entails psychical *consequences*. This way, we become more attuned to the consideration of the dynamics that take place in the ongoing psychic (re)construction of subjectivity through the use of language.

A serious consideration of this situation cannot but bring to the surface the often inhibited reality of anxiety, the underlying symptomatic structure that, for Freud, has come to define modern life, and the situation of education, for Britzman. It is precisely this indeterminacy revealed by psychoanalysis that renders our thinking about education problematic, as it lays bare our deeply held wishes, fantasies and desires, threatening to expose our fears, frustrations, resistances, repressions and the various defense mechanisms we so often employ to dress the narcissistic wound of the impossibility of our work in education: activism, rationalization, intellectualization, practicality, deferment, forgetfulness. The appearance of defense mechanisms is a clear indication that the ego is trying to defend against discomfort and suffering.

This faces us with the difficult question Freud left for education, that of having to explore the relations between learning and suffering.

Missing Links in the Progressive Project: (Dis)Identifications and the Unconscious

The notion that curricular work affects and regulates the identity of those involved in the pedagogical relation is, of course, not new nor exclusive to post-structural and psychoanalytic approaches. Various traditions and lines of work informed by Critical Theory helped bring into consideration some fundamental aspects of the educational act that challenged traditional and technicized notions of curriculum, inviting a profound reconceptualization of curriculum. The understanding of education as a political act, the ideological nature of curriculum, the struggle of power relations in the everyday life of schooling, the embeddedness of school in the social, cultural and economic milieu, and the role of schooling in class reproduction are a few of the many insights that allowed an understanding of the workings of curriculum beyond the transmission of subject matter, which then congealed in a scholarship of identity politics and revolutionary dissidence.[3]

---

[3] See, for example, James Kirylo's. (2013). "A Critical Pedagogy of Resistance: 34 Pedagogues We Need to Know".

Calls for a meaningful pedagogical practice, sustained by the hopes for social justice, inspired in radical social change, and articulated in direct action are certainly enticing and appealing for any teacher committed with an emancipatory project. It is perhaps due to a certain sense of responsibility, Taubman (2011) asserts, that educators are often found wanting to "do something now" and rushing to "turn any theory into practice" since they often "measure theory by its use value in the classroom" (p. 58). But to what extent can the discourse of structural macro categories of the social and the economic effectively and sustainably interpellate the individual subject? Or even more, attempt to produce a sense of personal identification? As we will see, *identification* is one of the fundamental psychic processes by which the subject defines the kind of relation it establishes with the other (or an image of the other, through fantasy, memories, and ideas). It is also a process through which the subject is himself constituted, and as such, an important element for our exploration of subjective reconstruction.

In the symptomatic compulsion to act (and to repeat), the progressive and critical agendas (such as the professionalization agenda, the social justice agenda, among others) appear to ignore crucial aspects of the subjectivity of both students and teachers. Following Taubman (2011), "social reconstructionists, in their focus on radical social change, marginalized a consideration of the psychic dimensions of social life...muffling the more radical insights, questioning and theory of freedom found in psychoanalysis" (p. 85). Some of the foci of attention that differentiate a psychoanalytically informed practice from that of progressives, are what make up an approach to curricular work that is attentive to the exploration of daily existence in terms of its "pain, violence, boredom, frustrations, terrors, dreams, desires, illogic, repetitions and obsessions" (Taubman 2011, p. 124).[4] In short, and by bringing the content of unconscious material to the fore, a psychoanalytic perspective of curriculum acknowledges as a starting point the most primal condition of humankind: that of suffering in the process of being and becoming.

---

[4]This is a central element in the diagnosis that Norbert Lechner (2002) does of Chilean civil society after the violent US intervention in the country in the 70s. Neoliberal democracy's failure to represent people in their fears and dreams help explain societal disaffection for civic participation.

Since "pragmatism was not interested in the foundational topics Freud had raised", Taubman (2011, p. 61) reminds us, traditional progressive and critical pedagogues could not see that the identifications they sought to achieve in the public by "telling it like it is" or the call to action can produce at the same the opposite effect: dis-identifications. Looking back on my own biographic trajectory, I can recognize elements that led up to a growing sense of dis-identification with assumptions of critical pedagogy to which I held firmly since my undergraduate education. Perhaps my moving away from the discourse of traditional critical theory, which marked my origins at a Jesuit university sometimes referred to as a "communist university", can be grasped psychoanalytically as the inevitable and necessary repudiation of the image of the father in the process of individuation, building new identifications for the subsequent reconstruction of subjectivity. A very short, though superficial, example of such dis-identification can be found in the insisting discourse of "resistance" in critical pedagogy. I had not become aware of the implications of the use of the notion until a colleague that worked with me in the curricular design of a nation-wide school program brought it to my attention: "*The word resistance seems to appear a lot in your speech. Don't you find it exhausting to live life resisting all the time?*". The question and the reflection on its implications stuck with me long after the initial shock and perplexity.

It was only after that informal analytic intervention that I came to learn from Argentinian philosopher Walter Mignolo that resistance "simply validates the existence of the norm, so instead of resisting, the ethical task is to re-exist. Critical pedagogues tend to focus on resistance", but psychoanalysis shows that what we resist, persists. That is precisely what happens in therapeutic practice when dealing only at the level of the symptom: the suppression of one symptom can only assure the reappearance of subjective conflict in the form of another symptom.

Is perhaps the instability of interpellation and the failure to create identifications in subjectivity that explain in part the fact that the project to educate "critically transformative" and "reflective practitioners" remains largely an "unrealized promise"? (Russell 2014). I share in Taubman's discomfort with identity politics, in that they have failed to recognize the unconscious, and with it, the understanding that "resistance to identity is at the heart of psychic life" (2011, p. 161).

Ignoring the psychoanalytic constitution of subjectivity in its core dimensions of desire, libidinal ties, suffering, and anxiety cannot go without consequences in the formative enterprise of curriculum work. Britzman (2003b) cites Donald Winnicott when in a talk given to policymakers in 1965 titled "The Price of Disregarding Psychoanalytic Research", he points to a fateful consequence also raised by Carl Jung: "We pay the price of just staying as we are, playthings of economics and of politics and of fate" (p. 110). The discursive revolutionary impulse in important part of the critical movement was also met by this warning when Jacques Lacan addressed the students in the Paris protests of 1968: "What you aspire to as revolutionaries is a new master. You will get one".

In what could be seen as a reconciling effort to bridge the tension between the insights of psychoanalysis and the progressive and critical project, William Pinar (2006) asserts that in order to resuscitate the progressive project in both subjective and social terms, we need "to understand that self-realization and democratization are inextricably intertwined" (p. 2) and in this effort, curriculum scholars "must renew our commitment to the democratization of…society, a pedagogical process that requires the psycho-social and intellectual development of the subjectively existing individual" (pp. 2–3).

Interestingly, as history shows, not all the left-wing and critical theorist have disavowed the subjectively existing individual or rejected pure theoretical work as bourgeois or narcissistic. As Taubman (2011) notices, the work of Frankfurt School scholar Herbert Marcuse demonstrates a strong commitment to the emancipatory project of psychoanalysis. In spite of the accusations from fellow Frankfurt School scholars, such as Eric Fromm, of "neglecting the practical", Marcuse sought to explore the philosophical and sociological implications of Freudian concepts, aiming "…not at curing individual sickness, but at diagnosing the general disorder" (Marcuse in Eros and Civilization, cited in Taubman 2011, p. 152). In contrast, he found the urgency for practical solutions in his colleagues to be "complicit with the rein of instrumental rationality and blind to the unconscious conflicts that render such gestures at best suspect" (p. 152).

The atrocities of technocratic mentality expressed throughout modern times (such as the Nazi regime, or the violent intervention in Chile to overthrow the democratically elected socialist government in the 70s and turn the country into a laboratory of neoliberal policies) left Critical scholars shocked and perplexed. Facing such horrors and hopeless times, for some it was time to recognize the danger of an action-oriented mentality, and ultimately, the impossibility of idealistic grand utopias. Taubman would agree with such sentiment, as he sees that one of the implications of psychoanalysis for curriculum is that it puts us in a situation where "we must accept our own complicity in the realities we discover in the classroom" (2011, p. 172).

In this sense, Deborah Britzman's claim is timely: "the approach that can best turn education inside out", in the interrogation of our complicit intentions and "...to understand its inhibitions, symptoms, and anxieties, is psychoanalysis" (2009, p. viii). It is to the exploration of these issues expressed in curricular work that we now turn.

Curriculum as a Site of Transference

The dynamics encountered in clinical experience with patients who exhibited varying processes of progress, and resistance to it, based on the relationship between analyst and analysand, led Freud to formulate what would become one of the organizing principles in the exploration of the unconscious: the notion of the transference. In his 1949 "Outline of Psychoanalysis", Freud explains it this way: in analysis "the patient sees in his analyst the return...of some important figure out of this childhood or past, and transfers on to him feelings and reactions that undoubtedly applied to this model.... This transference is ambivalent: it comprises positive and affectionate as well as negative and hostile attitudes towards the analyst" (p. 66).

In what sounds as a familiar scene to anybody who has taught (the relationship between analyst and analysand resembling that of teacher and student), notice how the ambivalence with which Freud defines this relationship also speaks to the "incalculability" of the pedagogical act referred to by Phelan earlier in this chapter. The relation with the pedagogical is confirmed in the educational attributes that Jacques Lacan confers to the relation of transference. In Seminar XI he indicates that "as soon as the subject who is supposed to know exists somewhere there is transference" (p. 232). Knowledge then becomes a central aspect in this relationship, and it occurs only when patient or student recognizes in the analyst or teacher the figure of a subject who is supposed to know. Transference, then, can be said to be the quintessential and identifying trait of the relationship between an analyst and the analysand, and between teacher and student.

The dialogic nature and decisive implication of curriculum work in the (re)construction of subjectivity by means of the transference can be inferred from the definition of transference and effect attributed to it in Lacan: "in its essence...transference...is quite simply the speech act. Each time a man speaks to another in an authentic and full manner there is, in the true sense, transference... something takes place which changes the nature of the two beings present" (Lacan, Seminar I, p. 109).

An important aspect that helps explain the potency of the transference is that even though it operates by means of the symbolic, or what can be accounted for at least in retrospect, it activates the unconscious, and with it, what cannot always be accounted for. The result is not superficial (cognitive) nor unidirectional: it changes the subjectivity of the two (or more) present. Having established the transformative effect in the subjects involved in a pedagogical situation by means of the transference, the question for the psychic dynamics involved in that process remains.

THE IMAGINARY AND THE FORMATION OF THE SUBJECT

In the Lacanian framework, subjectivity is understood in the interplay between three registers: the Real, the Imaginary, and the Symbolic.[5] In general terms, the register of the Real is where desires, passions, *jouissance*, and drives are located, along with everything that is unspeakable. The register of the Imaginary is the seat for the ego, which comprises both conscious and unconscious processes, such as memory, defenses, and judgment. The register of the Symbolic is the place of language, the capacity of representation. This register impacts on the other two.

In the process of formation of the I (or the Freudian ego, which is located within the), Lacan gives special attention to the psychical phenomenon of identification, or the capacity to locate ourselves in the other and to represent ourselves. This function of identification takes place in relation to the presence and mediation of an image. Following Lacan, identification is an inaugural process in the formation of subjectivity that starts in early childhood (the mirror stage and the recognition

---

[5] Lacan's framework of subjectivity also follows a tripartite model, just as the topology of the psyche in Freud. The Freudian psychical apparatus is formed, as the reader will recall, by the Id, the Ego, and the Super Ego. The Ego (in charge of self-preservation) is continuously in a position of having to reconcile the demands of the Id (drives and instincts) and the Super Ego (sense of obligations). In such relation of mediation, in which the Ego actively tries to seek pleasure and avoid unpleasure, tensions are bound to emerge.

of ourselves) and continues throughout life by the formative presence of subsequent specular images and the recognition of the other. The formative effect of the symbolic image is stated by Lacan when he describes identification as "the transformation that takes place in the subject when he assumes an image..." (Écrits, p. 76). In this sense, the images with which we are faced provide the Gestalt, or a vision of unity that allow us to assert ourselves in individuality. In the understanding that the image is symbolic in nature, that is, expressed in language, there is a real question about how we go about creating an image of ourselves, as it carries significant implications for the understanding of the curricular act.

In "The Subversion of the Subject and the Dialectics of Desire in the Freudian Unconscious" (1960), Lacan tells us that the process of ego construction is imaginary in nature and proposes that the circuit of identification "goes from the specular image to the constitution of the ego along the path of subjectification by the signifier..." (Écrits, p. 685). This presupposes a couple of crucial elements for the theorizing of curriculum. One of them, is that the process of subject formation occurs by the action of signifiers—language, words—that is, a symbolic act. The other, is that despite the initiation of the process of subjection in the register of the symbolic, the impact of its action (or its psychic consequences, in Britzman's words) are decided on a completely different register: that of the imaginary, as it interpellates the ego to assume a particular subject position.

What the curricular discourse of higher education does is precisely this: it constructs an image of a certain professional subject through a linguistic representation in program descriptions, graduate profiles, frames of competencies, course syllabi, evaluation and assessment, and classroom interactions, to which students are expected to strive to resemble.

But the process is far from being linear and straightforward. As we saw earlier, the same process by which we create identifications is the same one that brings about dis-identifications. Furthermore, and in what may seem a rather surprising insight at first, Lacan asserts that the image can simultaneously provoke passion but also oppression. This is because the image that we are presented (or that we construct for others) of a "good teacher" or an "exemplary parent", for example, is precarious, imaginary, and cannot really sustain our value, sense of dignity, and self-worth. The instant the image falters (which it will, due to its ethereal projection in the imaginary) it ends up being oppressive. As humans, we simply cannot continuously keep up a resemblance to an ideal image. This is a source of particular pain and suffering for the hysteric and the perfectionist (a trait of narcissism), many of which feel at home in the teaching profession.

The complexity of curricular work resides in the consequences it provokes at different registers of the psychic apparatus simultaneously: it operates in the symbolic, irrupting in the imaginary, while associating and struggling with and against the desires, libidinality, and traumas of the real. What is at stake in curriculum then is the formation of the subject.

The choice of the word "formation" here is not by chance, as it certainly was not in Lacan's vocabulary. Dylan Evans (1996) explains the difference between the English term "training" (as in teacher training) and the Latin term for "formation": "Whereas the English term carries connotations of a formal programme, or a bureaucratic structure, [formation] connotes a process which alters the subject in the very kernel of his being, and which cannot be regulated by set ritualistic procedures nor guaranteed by a printed qualification" (p. 213).

Since curriculum alters the subject at such depth, it is necessary to contemplate some considerations regarding the very notion of subject in relation to the pedagogical/analytical act. In her psychoanalytic investigations in education, in 1998 Deborah Britzman found herself "wondering about pedagogy's capacity to address the ego" (in Pinar, 1998, p. 321), quite possibly moved by the very important functions of the ego, such as perception and reality testing. In this sense, for Britzman, the ego and education share in common a constitutional ambivalence between change and adaptation.

Jacques Lacan, however, does not equate the ego with the subject, and in fact places them in different registers: the ego with its conscious sense of agency within the register of the imaginary, and the subject within the symbolic order (Evans 1996). This way, Lacan seems to be stripping the subject of conscious calculations, as he equates the subject with the subject of the unconscious. In its symbolic character, the subject is an effect of language (Écrits, p. 708). Writing almost a decade later, Britzman would seem to agree: "…education requires association, interpretation and a narrative capable of bringing to awareness, for further construction, things that are farthest from the mind" (2009, p. viii).

But it is in "The Subversion of the Subject" (1960) where Lacan presents the intriguing "graph of desire", defining the subject as the inextricable relation between signifier and desire. In demonstrating this intricate constitution of the subject, he opened the way to the understanding of the subject as a "speaking being" (*parlêtre*, in Lacan's terms), as primordially split, against the illusion of the unitary subject of psychology (desire is always the desire of or for the other), and the libidinal investments of desire in what we construct as knowledge.

The implications of these facts from analytic experience for curriculum are, of course, manifold. It is "the struggle for words", Britzman asserts, what "has as its pressure point the speaker's theory of language joined to erotic life", and in agreement with Lacan, suggests that "Listening for the Eros of language is a key contribution psychoanalysis brings to understanding the undercurrents of communication that do affect pedagogical exchange" (2014, pp. 123–124).

For Peter Taubman, working with the unconscious and desire is a pedagogical act of creation articulated with its temporal dimension: "…teaching becomes the creation of conditions for re-symbolizing and re-constructing alternative futures that lie in scattered looks, ideas, feelings, sensations, words, gestures but have not yet come into being" (2011, p. 187). In the dwelling in this "now but not yet", and in the struggle for words, we are confronted not only with the other, but with our own image—a source of suffering and anxiety—as we are faced with the fragility of the imaginary and the enslaving patterns of repetition of what remains unsaid.

In this conflictive process of formation of the subject, symptoms are bound to arise. It is to the exploration of this aspect faced in the analytic and curricular act that we now turn.

The Unfinished Symptom

> …education cannot proceed without anxiety, and this emotional fact presses on our first education, creating an archive of symptomology and dissolving its terms into unconscious ideation, repression, the compulsion to repeat and the return of the repressed. Deborah Britzman (2011, p. 128)

As we have discussed so far, the often unspoken reality of the curricular experience is that it throws us right into the drama of becoming. The process of subjective formation is one that is "suffered, dramatized, enacted" (Butler 2004, p. 45), and in the context of higher education, Britzman describes it as "the drama of human beings constructing their identities…in situations marked by tension between what seems given or inalterable and what may be perceived as possibility" (2003b, p. ix). A psychoanalytic view of education then has as starting point the acknowledgment of uneasiness, suffering, and discontent.

In this sense, we recognize that in the drama of having to educate and be educated, the pedagogical relation carries with it particular psychical consequences—that of symptoms, among which, for Britzman, anxiety is one that plagues all education.

But what do we talk about when we talk about symptoms? Dylan Evans (1996) explains that from a traditional perspective of medicine, symptoms are seen as "the perceptible manifestations of an underlying illness that might otherwise remain undetected" (p. 205).

While this view is predicated on a distinction between surface and a depth where causes "hide", Lacan changes the entire logic of the matter by demonstrating that the symptom belongs to the realm of the symbolic, that is, language. In a talk in 1953, Lacan asserts that the issue of symptoms "can be entirely resolved in an analysis of language, because a symptom it itself structured like a language" (Ècrits, p. 223). The implications are manifold. The distinction between surface/depth in the traditional approach to medicine is superseded, as language is always present right there "at the surface", open to interpretation.

Following Lacan, "a symptom can only be interpreted in the signifying order". It is an articulation of something else, since "a signifier has meaning only through its relation to another signifier" (p. 194). From this perspective, a symptom is a word trapped in the body.

This is why Lacan insists that "a symptom is language from which speech must be delivered" (Ècrits, p. 223), a position shared by Freud as he referred to symptoms as "meaning being suffered" (Britzman 2011, p. 31).

A practical illustration of this from Lacan's clinical experience is the case of a woman he treated who was afflicted with Astasia-Abasia (being unable to move or walk without assistance or support). After several months in which she resisted several therapeutic approaches, Lacan identified the image that marked her discourse: that of her father. As he recounts it, the outcome of the finding came with the deliverance of meaning: "…it was enough for me to remark that she had not had [her father's] support…for her to be cured of her symptom" (Ècrits, p. 88).

As an object of interpretation, the symptom is a signifier with no universal meaning (Evans 1996). The non-universality of meaning attributed to the chain of signifiers operating in the transference in the pedagogical relation leads me to suggest the theorization of curriculum in terms of its function as catalyst in an unfinished symptom.

I recognize a commonality between analysis and pedagogy (apart from the fact that both were identified as the "impossible professions" by Freud), in that—as Lacan indicates—"psychoanalytic action", as well as pedagogical action, "develops in and through verbal communication, that is, in a dialectical grasping of meaning" (Ècrits, p. 83). Being a meaning-making practice, curriculum always implies the making of a subject, since as Lacan suggested, "every meaning phenomenon implies a subject" (ibid.). In this dialectic, the understanding and attribution of a meaning is constructed differently by each subject involved in the relation.

In this sense, the completion of the response to the signifiers/images provided in the pedagogical relation set up by curriculum is marked by a hallmark trait: its unpredictability.

Our need to constantly respond and complete the symptom is predicated on our own sense of incompleteness, of being split right from the moment of weaning, the sense of loss that comes thereafter, and the constitution of our desire in terms of the desire of the other.

Britzman (2009) seems to be pointing to this as she discusses education as both interminable and impossible: "education itself will be interminable because it is always incomplete, and because it animates our own incompleteness" (p. 3).

Being a (complicated) conversation as it is, the psychical responses with which we take part in the dialectic of the curricular situation are varied.

As mentioned earlier, Deborah Britzman identifies anxiety, along with inhibitions, as common completions of the symptom initiated in the pedagogical relation (2014). In what appears to be a shared diagnosis, Taubman (2011) also references work that identifies anxiety as an "essential topic" to be addressed in teacher education programs (p. 108).

Under today's obsession with the specification and standardization of practices and outcomes in higher education, one could see how the unpredictability in a true pedagogical act may be a source of anxiety for those who wish to control it. Referring to the impossibility of education Britzman indicates that "...however good and intentional our methods may feel, we cannot guarantee, for either ourselves or others, the force, experience, or interpretation of our efforts once they become events in the world of others" (2003b, p. 16).

Within the Freudian structure of the psychical apparatus (Id, Ego, and Superego), anxiety is a symptom that originates in the Ego. As we have seen, this is also the space where important part of the psychical consequences of the curricular act are felt and get sedimented.

Since the task of the Ego is to pursue pleasure (in complicity with the instincts of the Id) while at the same time avoiding unpleasure (defending against the moral impositions and castigation from the Superego), any increase of unpleasure is met with the signal of anxiety (Freud 1949). Since the main purpose of the Ego is self-preservation, anything that is perceived as a danger to the present configuration of the self as it is will trigger the Ego's deployment of a series of defense mechanisms. Examples of some of these are rationalization (one of the main forms of resistance "against psychoanalytic insights), repression, projection, sublimation, forgetfulness, and even late arrivals to sessions/classes are counted as an aggressive form" of resistance and evasion (Lacan 1948 in Écrits 2006). Anxiety then, is ultimately an expression of conflict, and a clear indication of a sense of threat to a familiar configuration and stability of the self.

In this sense, it is not surprising that any education—particularly higher education—would bring about anxiety, where there is lots at stake. But why is it that anxiety and other similar expressions of discomfort do not seem to be only prevalent, but actually a defining trait that characterizes the process of teacher education in modern times? (Britzman 2003a).

This is a similar question to the one raised by Freud (1949) when he asked why neurotics—in spite of having the same innate dispositions as other people, the same experiences and the same problems to solve—seem to live so much worse, with greater difficulty, and suffer more feelings of unpleasure, anxiety, and pain. His answer goes along the idea of disharmonies and disorders in the Ego. At first sight, it could be said that people with artistic/creative capacities and those who choose to become teachers share a similar psychological structure: that of the neurotic. But there is more to the reason of the increased suffering.

As we said, in its consideration of safety and self-preservation, the ego guards itself in its function of reality-testing using anxiety as a signal of danger threatening its integrity. In this sense, the completion of the symptom in the form of strong anxiety experienced by those in the process of becoming teachers, as well as by their educators (something not experienced quite as much in other occupations, such as engineering) could be evidence of the deep process of transformation of not only cognitive structures, but of the self. This is why the ego interprets pedagogical situations as processes that threaten its current familiar configuration and balance.

Although Lacan also refers to issues of the ego, his approach is more nuanced, warning against the temptation to strengthen the ego, and thus making the person more adaptable to society. In one of his early papers from 1948, Lacan suggests that the ego is constituted by two categories, i.e. the spatial and the temporal, and places anxiety as a symptomatic phenomenon of the temporal (Écrits 2006, p. 89). I am inclined to believe that a reason for his view of anxiety as a temporal phenomenon can be explained by his understanding of the symptom as an expression of conflicting desires. In the Rome Discourse (1953), he asserts that the symbols of the symptom express the language of desire. As we know, desire is by definition metonymic. It never remains the same and never accomplishes what it supposedly desires. It continuously moves along an endless chain of signifiers.

As with other temporal phenomena, symptoms derived from anxiety can also be recurring. At the same time, they do not always remain as a privately felt discomfort and show up externally in discursive manifestations, such as teachers' constant pattern of judging ideas on their use value. This is something that Deborah Britzman brings to attention: comments such as ""it is nice in theory but not in the real world" … may well represent unfinished symptoms that defend against the more difficult question of what happens when our pedagogy is caught somewhere between ignorance and knowledge, between not knowing what to do and still having to act…" (2003b, p. 75).

As an unfinished symptom, the images/signifiers put in play by the curricular situation will provoke incalculable responses in students as they finish up the symptom, as informed by their biographies, existential meanings attributed to the situation and the psychological structure prevalent in their psycho-somatic life.

Curriculum and the Flowing of Transference

As imaginary work, the images curriculum constructs for those in the pedagogical situation are unstable, phantasmatic, and precarious, and as such, they cannot always sustain a subject's notion of self, let alone produce identifications with it in predictable ways. It is in part the frustration produced by the incalculability of the pedagogical encounter that experience confirms that throws us in constant efforts to change, update, or better describe the image(s) we provide, through (re)definitions of standards of practice, course contents, syllabi descriptions, statements of outcomes, or criteria for assessment and evaluation.

The issue then is what happens next, after the confirmation of the presence of a myriad of different symptoms completed by both teachers and students in the environment of interpellations, identifications and dis-identifications set off by the curricular situation.

Even though the emancipatory project of psychoanalysis is not interested in curing the symptom, in the same way, an emancipatory approach to education is not interested in curing ignorance (Taubman 2011), both education and analysis are, as Lacan emphasized, an act.

In the understanding that anxiety and all its related symptoms and defenses derive from the ego, a popular approach has been to find ways to strengthen the ego. In this effort, what is deemed as a faulty image is attempted to be replaced by a different one, usually by way of positive reinforcement of the individual ("you can do it", "cheer up", "pull yourself together"). Ego psychology and behaviorism have profited immensely from this approach. However, this is an imaginary "solution": the seat of the image and the ego-ideal is the register of the imaginary, and as we have discussed, we cannot be sustained in the long run by it. Lacan attacked these approaches, pointing not only to the oppressive potential of the image, but also reminding that strengthening the ego can only help it succeed in its purpose: promoting the (safe but stagnant) social adaptation of the individual. This is clearly not the point of the emancipatory project of the analytic act. For this reason, in the rather radical conference of "The Subversion of the Subject" (1960) Lacan denounces psychology's "lowly purposes of social exploitation" (Ècrits, p. 676).

A different approach, one more in sync with a psychoanalytic view of education, is to move in the opposite direction, away from the imaginary of the ego and into the realm of the symbolic. The point is to get teachers and students to ground and assert themselves in language, speaking not from a specular image in the imaginary (the ideal or normative view of how things should be, or what they think is expected from them) but from the Real (the drives, their desires).

In a certain way, this movement reminds of what Socrates did with his students, undoing speculative images through constant and open questioning, pushing the limits of what seemed granted.

While traditional approaches to curriculum influenced by ego psychology and other forms of technical rationality focus their efforts in getting individuals to adhere to a certain image or ego-ideal, psychoanalytic experience has shown that the investment and fixation of libidinal energy within the self (itself a form of narcissism) brings about illness not only expressed in internal psychic disturbance, but also oftentimes in somatic manifestations. The treatment of paralyses or recurring fainting through psychoanalytic confrontation attest to this. Peter Taubman cites the Hungarian psychoanalyst Sándor Ferenczi, who warned that education was "literally a forcing house for various neuroses" (Ferenczi 1994 in Taubman 2011, p. 47).

In contrast, a liberatory approach sees the need to keep that libidinal energy flowing from the inside out; a movement that calls for real and authentic transference, that is, it requires conversation. This is one of the reasons why psychoanalysis is often referred to as the "talking cure". In the light of the implications of a Lacanian perspective of the transference, perhaps the most beneficial purpose to which curriculum workers can give themselves to is, instead of making efforts to fixate energy in attaining a certain predefined image or ego-ideal, to engage in a practice that keeps the transference flowing, a practice in which free association allows for repressed material and desire in the unconscious to be liberated.

Curriculum theorist Dwayne Huebner also describes the potency of conversation in the pedagogical relation. "In conversation", he asserts, "we are significantly changed… reality is found, solitude transcended, and life shaped" (1999, p. 80). The transformative potential of conversation adduced by Huebner certainly finds sustain in the etymology of the term. In its Latin roots conversation derives from the components *Com* (with) and *Versare* (to turn). This way, conversation can be loosely translated as "to change together".

This is the type of conversation Lacan has in mind when he says that transference happens every time people speak in a full and authentic manner. Conversation that allows for the flow of transference differs dramatically from the instrumental use of talk in the classroom that teachers incorporate as a strategy to get students to do or learn something (Huebner 1999).

In considering the performative effect of curriculum in the ongoing (re)configuration of the subject through a use of language that appears as an unfinished symptom, psychoanalysis opens the invitation to rethink received and familiar notions and, in so doing, reimagine the possibilities of joining in a conversation that, acknowledging our sufferings and desires of the Real, can lead us in the subjective reconstruction of more honest and authentic lives.

References

Bracher, M. (1993). *Lacan, Discourse and Social Change: A Psychoanalytic Cultural Criticism*. New York: Cornell University Press.

Britzman, D. (1998). On Some Psychical Consequences of AIDS Education. In W. Pinar (Ed.), *Queer Theory in Education* (pp. 265–277). Abingdon: Routledge.

Britzman, D. (2003a). *Practice Makes Practice: A Critical Analysis of Learning to Teach*. Albany, NY: SUNY Press.

Britzman, D. (2003b). *After-Education: Anna Freud, Melanie Klein, and Psychoanalytic Histories of Learning*. Albany, NY: SUNY Press.

Britzman, D. (2009). *The Very Thought of Education: Psychoanalysis and the Impossible Professions*. Albany, NY: SUNY Press.

Britzman, D. (2011). *Freud and Education*. New York, NY: Routledge.

Britzman, D. (2014). That Other Scene of Pedagogy: A Psychoanalytic Narrative. *Changing English, 21*(2), 122–130.

Butler, J. (2004). *The Judith Butler Reader* (S. Salih, Ed.). Malden: Blackwell.

Da Silva, T. (2001). *Espacios de Identidad: Nuevas visiones sobre el currículum*. Barcelona: Octaedro.

Evans, D. (1996). *An Introductory Dictionary of Lacanian Psychoanalysis*. New York, NY: Routledge.

Freud, S. (1949). *An Outline of Psychoanalysis*. New York: W. W. Norton.

Freud, S. (1957). *Civilization and Its Discontents*. London: Hogarth Press.

Grimmett, P., & Halvorson, M. (2010). From Understanding to Creating Curriculum: The Case for the Co-Evolution of Re-Conceptualized Design with Re-Conceptualized Curriculum. *Curriculum Inquiry, 40*(2), 241–262.

Huebner, D. (1999). *The Lure of the Transcendent. Collected Essays by Dwayne E. Huebner* (W. Pinar & V. Ellis, Eds.). New York: Routledge.
Kirylo, J. (Ed.). (2013). *A Critical Pedagogy of Resistance: 34 Pedagogues We Need to Know*. Rotterdam,The Netherlands: Sense Publishers.
Lacan, J. (2006). *Écrits: The First Complete Edition in English* (B. Fink, Trans.). New York: W. W. Norton.
Lechner, N. (2002). *Las sombras del mañana: La dimensión subjetiva de la política*. Santiago: LOM ediciones.
Phelan, A. (2010). "Bound by Recognition": Some Thoughts on Professional Designation for Teachers. *Asia-Pacific Journal of Teacher Education, 38*(4), 317–329.
Pinar, W. (2006). *The Synoptic Text Today and Other Essays: Curriculum Development After the Reconceptualization*. New York: Peter Lang.
Pinar, W., Reynolds, W., Slattery, P., & Taubman, P. (1995). *Understanding Curriculum: An Introduction to the Study of Historical and Contemporary Curriculum Discourses*. New York: Peter Lang.
Russell, T. (2014). Paradigmatic Changes in Teacher Education: The Perils, Pitfalls, and the Unrealized Promise of the "Reflective Practitioner". In R. Bruno-Jofré & J. S. Johnston (Eds.), *Teacher Education in a Transnational World* (pp. 158–176). Toronto: University of Toronto Press.
Taubman, P. (2011). *Disavowed Knowledge: Psychoanalysis, Education and Teaching*. New York: Routledge.

CHAPTER 3

Critique: Between Theory and Method

Abstract This chapter proposes a method of psychoanalytic critique of curriculum. This critique considers the ways in which the ego mediates symptomatically between the demands for adaptation, resistance, and change. The examination of curricular discourse as symptom carries particular significance for the understanding of the processes of self-discovery and formation. The chapter is organized in three sections. The first one offers a discussion of a general concept of critique. The second one delves into central tenets of Lacanian psychoanalysis and attempts the development of an apparatus of elements for a psychoanalytic critique of curriculum. The chapter closes with a discussion of implications of such form of critique for the conceptualization and investigation of curriculum as a form of educational research.

Keywords Critique · Symptom · Method · Lacanian psychoanalysis
Educational research

INTRODUCTION

To some, bringing together psychoanalysis and education might seem an odd combination, if not one that can be perceived with a hint of reluctance, unease, or in the best case, with intrigue, as Peter Taubman assesses in his study of the history of the relationship between these two practices (Taubman 2011). But the affinity between the psychoanalytic and the curricular act is manifold. For one, both analysis and pedagogy were identified by Freud as impossible professions. Though a central notion to the understanding of their workings, their compatibility goes beyond that.

The investigative practice in curriculum, as a complex and heterogeneous field, involves the identification and delimitation of an area to be examined. Such a field that concerns research in curriculum studies, for Pinar (1975), is an educational experience. Within this field, Britzman (2009) zooms in an area that highlights a more specific problem that speaks of the affinity of education and analysis: the psychoanalytic problem of "trying to understand the expressions and symbolizations of internal plurality" (p. 118). This internal plurality, though originated in the quotidian interaction with the (M)Other, is systematically interpellated and transformed in the deliberate and intentional efforts carried out in the institutionalized practice of both education and psychotherapy.

In this sense, both analysis and pedagogy are an *act*, a term that carried particular significance for Lacan, as they involve a dynamic, movement and intentionality. Though the educative work of analysis (and the analytical work of education) is sustained in words, they are nonetheless a form of intervention. They carry real, imaginary and symbolic consequences.

As I claimed in the previous chapter, these consequences operate in curricular work as unfinished symptoms. As these psychical (and in occasions somatic) dynamics operate in symbolic forms, i.e. through words, we recognize the centrality of language, and in particular, the signifier. Britzman presents this position plainly yet poignantly: "Freud is the writer for people who want to find out what words may have done to them, and may still be doing" (2009, p. vii). Though symptoms and their etiology can only be looked at in retrospective, a psychoanalytic critique of curriculum looks at the material traces of its discourse, the marks of desire and assumptions, that constitute elements that appear as unfinished symptoms, ready to elicit their completion by the other. As we will see, a psychoanalytic critique of curriculum involves the consideration of curriculum in its dimension of language but also temporality.

Historically, there has been a line of incisive criticism that has delved into the conditions of schooling and their effects on the *lebenswelt* of those who inhabit the educational world (Pinar 1975). Though approached from different angles and traditions, such investigations seem to arrive at a shared conclusion, one that is articulated most eloquently by William Pinar's excellent paper "Sanity, Madness and School" (1975): modern schooling is not only dehumanizing. It is maddening.

This investigation, situated within this historical lineage of reconceptualized character, advances an approach to criticism of curriculum from the vantage point of psychoanalytic theory. That is, a form of critique that does not focus exclusively on the exteriority of perceived lived experience (which can be a product of alienation and ideological distortion) but on the psychic dynamics involved in the manifestations of the unconscious and the ways through which the ego mediates symptomatically between the invitation and demands for adaptation, resistance, and change.

The theoretical base of this study is Lacanian psychoanalysis (a continuation of the work of Freud), which represents not only a therapeutic but also a philosophical analytical practice that addresses unconscious content and underlying structures of experience. In the effort to delineate an approach to criticism in the field of curriculum studies, I rely mainly on the work of William Pinar and Deborah Britzman, whose work is distinctly marked and informed by a psychoanalytic understanding of subjectivity, engaging in a dialogue of juxtapositions with others who have contributed importantly to understanding curriculum as a plural text with decisive implications.

I claim that in the context of the curricular situation of higher education, the examination of its discourses as symptoms carry particular significance for the understanding of the process of self-discovery and formation as a subject.

As the famous quote attributed to Carl Jung notes, the stakes are high: "unless you make the unconscious conscious, it will continue to direct your life, and you will call it fate". Though in different words, Pinar expresses a similar sentiment when, discussing the need for curricular criticism, he asserts that "without proper theoretical grounding...we ask the wrong questions" and in turn, we end up "forced to accept a logic that oppresses us" (1975, pp. 417–418).

For the curricular worker, the challenge of such kind of critique is, in part, having to suspend the tendency to act based on interpretations of discourses and actions as they appear, and instead, take them as what they are: symbolic representations of something else. This involves the effort of making facile gestures difficult, through the interpretive stance of turning the gaze inwards and listening carefully to the demands and desires of the Other asking, as Lacan suggested, "*What do you want?*" and "*What do you want from me?*".

In outlining a response to the question "What is psychoanalytic critique?" in the field of curriculum, this chapter is organized into three broad sections. The first one deals with a brief discussion of a general concept of critique. The second one delves into central tenets of psychoanalysis and attempts the development of an apparatus of elements for a psychoanalytic critique of curriculum. The paper closes with a discussion of implications of such form of critique for the conceptualization and investigation of curriculum.

The 'Critical' Element in Critique

Criticality can be thought of as an "attitude", a form of work sustained in a particular stance towards the world that is brought about by the encounter with human arrangements that are oppressive, unjust, or that generate discontent and suffering. It was perhaps such an encounter with suffering that led the British playwright Alan Bennett to dig deeper into the intricacies of the pedagogical relationship between teacher and student in his play *The History Boys*. In its introduction, as he recounts his personal biographical experiences as a background for the story, he mentions noticing in teachers the existence of "secret sorrows" and recalls a particular event that led him to an unexpected realization: "*Once in a slack period of the afternoon when we were being particularly un-bright, the French master put his head down on the desk and wailed, 'Why am I wasting my life in this god-forsaken school?' ... The incident stuck in my mind...because it was a revelation to me at the time...that masters had inner lives (or lives at all)*" (2004, p. xii).

Although important part of the work done in cultural criticism started to ignore and disavow the significance of focusing on issues of inner life and the psychical and social consequences of cultural artifacts in those who consume them, Mark Bracher suggests that, at a general level, all critical activities take their value "from the difference they make in people's lives" (1993, p. 1). This attitude and disposition of making a difference, of promoting some sort of transformation that could eventually lead to greater freedom, can be traced (at least in modern times) back to the particular character imprinted to the critical interest in the work of intellectuals associated to the Frankfurt School. For Jürgen Habermas, the distinctive characteristic of critical forms of knowledge is their orientation towards emancipation. This particular character is also strongly present in the work of Max Horkheimer. In the introduction to the Spanish edition of his *Traditional and Critical Theory*, Jacobo Muñoz comments that for Horkheimer "the critical theorist is, in effect, the one whose work consists in accelerating a process that must lead to a society without injustice. That to whose work underlies a qualified emancipatory interest" (2000, p. 21). Emancipation, for Habermas, has to do with "independence from everything that is outside the individual" (1972, p. 205). One may wonder here what happens with oppressive structures and patterns that are inside the individual, but we will turn to that shortly. A critical interest aims, fundamentally, at the liberation of human beings from the diverse forms of oppression and domination that act in, on, and through us, limiting our self-determination and subjecting certain groups to the acceptance of a system that denies them an interesting and satisfactory life. In other words, a critical attitude takes the side of those who suffer, the disadvantaged, the misrepresented, the misfits, the excluded.

The Art of not Being Governed so Much

The development of the critical attitude in the Western world is traced from the fifteenth century in the historical study that Michel Foucault does in his piece "What is critique?" (1997). Rather than connected to a specific task, the critical attitude is—for Foucault—akin to virtue, as it is not directed only at eradicating error, but more generally, it represents a certain way of being with others and with ourselves: it encompasses ways of thinking, speaking, acting, and "a certain relationship to what exists, to what one knows…to society, to culture and also a relationship to others" (p. 42). From the different possible routes to examine the development of the critical attitude, Foucault chooses to focus on the ecclesiastical practices of the Roman and Greek Catholic church, as it provides rich antecedents for the emergence of critique. The efficacy of their action (through practices such as confessions or methods of examination) derives from what they called the *ars artium*, the direction of conscience, something that Foucault prefers to call the "art of governing men".

During the fifteenth and sixteenth century, coinciding with the expansion of the Spanish empire and the discovery of the New World, the fundamental question of the time, Foucault notes, was "How to govern". The art of governing men pervaded into a variety of areas, such as governing children, armies, cities, states, as well as bodies and minds. In this process, Foucault asserts that the big question of the time was answered by a multiplication of the arts of governing, including pedagogy, politics, and economics. It is then at the junction of the movement of governmentalization of both public and private life that the critical attitude emerges, asking "How not to be governed?". The critical attitude is, for Foucault, an "act of defiance, a challenge, as a way of limiting these arts of governing and seizing them up, transforming them, of finding a way to escape from them, or a way to displace them, with a basic mistrust" (p. 45). He then advances the first definition of critique: "the art of not being governed quite so much" (ibid.).

A central element subjacent to the arts of governing identified by Foucault is that they establish a particular relationship to truth, turning the issue of government and critique, in important ways, a problem of knowledge. This element becomes more apparent when he suggests three historical anchoring points in which the critical attitude is sustained:

First, when the art of governing men was essentially an ecclesiastic practice, critique appears as an act related to the use of the scriptures. As demonstrated in the movement initiated by Protestantism, the return to the scriptures to see what they really said in contrast to the church dogma, was a way of challenging and limiting the ecclesiastical rule. Historically, then, for Foucault "critique is biblical" (p. 46). This claim appears to be supported by the etymology of the term "critique". In its Latin derivation, it refers to an ability for discernment. In the work of Roman philosophers, such as Cicero, *criticus* is used to designate judgment of the works of the spirit.

Second, critique acquires a legal character as it appears as a will not to be governed. Not wanting to accept certain laws rest on the assessment that they are unjust and that they hide a fundamental illegitimacy. Exploring these hidden aspects and the limits of their efficacy require an interpretive and hermeneutic stance.

Third, the critical attitude appears when not accepting as true what authority claims is true. Acceptance of its terms derives only from the consideration of valid reasons to do so. This exercise also requires an epistemological orientation.

It must be noted here that, because of its stance and conviction, the critical attitude is not always tolerated by authority and can entail a dangerous endeavor. Recall the story of the English priest John Ball, who in a famous sermon preached in the 1380s declared:

> ...things cannot go right in England until all goods are held in common, and the lords are not greater masters than ourselves; We are all descended from Adam and Eve... [yet] they have handsome manors and houses and we the pain and travail, the rain and winds in the fields. And it is from our labor that they get the means to maintain their estates. Let us go to the king, and tell him we shall have it otherwise, or else we will provide a remedy ourselves.

Not long after this sermon John Ball was tried, hung, drawn, quartered and beheaded as a traitor.

The antecedents to the critical attitude provided by Foucault allow for the understanding of critique as a practice fundamentally involved and sustained in the interaction of the triad of power, knowledge (truth) and the subject.

Seen this way, critique has a pedagogical function. It illuminates the assumptions on which knowledge is presented as valid, and the power relations that, at once, make that presentation possible and create the conditions for individuals to assume a certain subject position. One can see, then, how emancipation—in a true critical attitude—encompasses far more than merely what is external to the individual, as Habermas suggested.

As curriculum also operates in the same triad, one where subjectivity is at stake, for William Pinar (2015), critique is a crucial practice of curriculum studies. In agreement with the attitude described by Foucault, Pinar asserts that critique implies "not only non-coincidence but reconstruction as questioning, skepticism, forming finally conviction" (p. 197). Methodologically, critique in curriculum studies is "informed by lived experience", though not taken as self-evident nor driven by whimsies of passions, but an intellectual exercise that is "juxtaposed with academic knowledge and compelled by conviction" (p. 197). The element of conviction resonates strongly with the Latin root of critique. The art of critiquing curriculum, in this sense, and because of its objects and implications, is an act of judgment: a practice of aesthetic appraisal, mediated by experience, and sustained in ideology.

Opposing Projects

In reconstructing the history of the relationship between psychoanalysis and education, Peter Taubman (2011) recognizes that not all approaches to the analytical and pedagogical act share the same understanding of their purpose, nor an orientation that guides their practice. As he suggests, the regard toward the unconscious and its effects is the central element that explains the split within these two impossible professions, giving place to the conformation of two different and opposing agendas, which he terms the therapeutic project and the emancipatory project.

In general terms, the analytical and pedagogical act guided by the therapeutic project is characterized by an effort to "cure" the patient-student of illness or ignorance. In this effort, the process is directed to the attainment of particular goals, such as a change in opinion or behavior. Taubman points out that even teachers or analysts who reject the behavioral-medical approaches to their practice, demonstrate a commitment to this project every time they orient themselves to reaching some sort of preset outcome, or give into the pragmatic compulsion to act, even when such commitments are directed to raising awareness of social inequalities or other noble pursuits of the like.

In contrast to the therapeutic project that, ultimately, disavows the unconscious, the emancipatory project is directed to an understanding of inner life, "without promising the result will be a happier…or more just life…or a higher test score" (Taubman 2011, pp. 6–7). Instead, it offers "questions and an interminable analysis, rather than answers and solutions" (p. 7). He further explains that the emancipatory project aspires to problematize taken-for-granted views of ourselves and others, bringing in a consideration of the unconscious with its desires, memories, and fears, and providing a theoretical orientation to the understanding and redirection of lived experience. As a critical practice, it "relies on a critical hermeneutic, but one that attends to its own desires, the unruliness of the body, and both the Eros and aggression of conscious and unconscious thought" (p. 28).

The distinctive element that delimitates one project from the other, then, is the critical attitude: emancipatory criticality can never foresee its results, nor expects to do so. For Zaretsky (2004), the North American version of psychoanalysis (and by extension, the pedagogical discourses that stemmed from it) eventually "became a method of cure and a form of self-improvement rather than a critical stance" (cited in Taubman 2011, p. 26).

What Does Psychoanalytic Critique Involve?

> "to rethink (...) that is my method" J. Lacan
> Seminar XIII

In conceptual work, one can very seldom know beforehand the method(s) through which insight comes about. It is a discovery in retrospect. One needs to look back at what one has done in order to retrace and reconstruct one's steps that led to new theorizations and understandings. In this sense, philosophical study is revealed in its sensitivity to temporality. In the difficulty that the institutionalized and positivistic academic establishment imposes for philosophical-conceptual work in having to conform and comply with traditional language-practices of methods (and their derived preoccupations such as data, technique, representativeness, validity, among many others), Claudia Ruitenberg (2009) acknowledges the problem but points out that philosophical work has not been without method, even when they do not fit into the pre-determined categories of the natural sciences.

Though focusing on a slightly different topic, William Doll—in a talk titled "Seeking for a method beyond a method" (2015)—shares Ruitenberg's concern with the "baggage", assumptions, expectations and demands that the traditions from which the notion of method is uttered bring to specific fields and modes of work. In the context of teacher education, Doll shows that the issue of method has not only been rendered an "assorted bag of tricks", but has also installed a product-oriented frame that "do not…open either teacher or student to the intricacies, mysteries, paradoxes, joys, and beauties of a subject". Further, he denounces, "methods…tacitly determine a frame of domination".

In asking the question for how might philosophical work be articulated in its own terms, describing the type of work it undertakes, while staying away from the "methodolatry" Rorty denounced and the domination that Doll exposed, Ruitenberg (2009) suggests thinking of method as "the various ways and modes in which philosophers of education think, read, write, speak and listen, that make their work systematic, purposeful and responsive to past and present philosophical and educational concerns and conversations" (p. 316). In short, she writes, bringing method into being comes by "naming [the] ways of thinking and writing" and thus making these ways of thinking and writing "available for explicit consideration" (p. 315).

This is to a large extent what can be seen across the work of Sigmund Freud and Jacques Lacan in the field of psychoanalysis, and William Pinar in curriculum studies (see for example Pinar 1975, 2006, 2015). None of them shied away from using the term method when referring to and describing the logics of their work. Method, after all, in its Greek root *methodos* is a path one traverses, and we are implicated in that walk right now.

For Jacques Lacan, his method, i.e. rethinking, was a form of commentary that—though heavily recursive—was organized, as he explains, with a guiding grid composed of a particular way of approaching elements of psychic dynamics that helped him think through the lived experiences of symptoms.

Provisionally, and at the present stage of this work, I propose an approach to psychoanalytic critique organized in a guiding grid of thought that brings together elements from psychoanalytic as well as curricular theory. This approach includes primordially the attention to linguistic utterances and the *enoncé* (i.e. the subject of the enunciation) as modeled in the work of both Freud and Lacan, in conjunction with the type of commentary organized in juxtaposition present primarily in the work of William Pinar and in Deborah Britzman.

In focusing not on the whole of discourse, but in bits that may trigger new insight (as Freud suggests in his discussion of method in the *Outline of Psychoanalysis*), this form of investigation would work as a synoptic analysis; that is, the presentation of critical commentary by juxtaposition of segments of discourse and theory that is relevant for insight into the object of this method: the processes of subjection through curricular discourse.

Approached as a form of study, this method of analysis shares in the rationale described by Pinar (1975) when he outlines a method for the analysis of educational experience: "The analyst of educational experience… attempts to discover what factors are operative in educational experience, what relations among what factors under what circumstances, and finally, what fundamental structures describe or explain the educative process" (p. 392). This outline, which he would soon after refine as the method of *Currere* as presented at the AERA that same year, reflects to a large extent the investigative stance of the work of Freud and Lacan, particularly when it comes to explaining the structures subjacent to what is perceived as experience. Recall here, for example, that a Lacanian approach looks at symptomatic formations as expressions of psychical structures. The focus, then, being on explaining the psychic dynamic that sets the stage for that symptom to appear, rather than describing the experience of the symptom itself.

The approach proposed here is similar to that of William Pinar and Deborah Britzman, in that it attends to the ways psychoanalysis affects our account of curricular activity and the very thought of education (Britzman 2010). In his methodological outline to investigating educational experience, Pinar suggests recollecting the past and sifting emotional components through intellect, affirming the need for consciousness. Though Lacan would agree that in certain cases the analytic process requires pulling the images of the ego to the realm of the symbolic (the intellectual use of language) for it to have a therapeutic effect, Freud reminds us that our memories and recollections of experience—as a by-product of the unconscious—are not that different from dream work: the presentation of meaning through metonymy, metaphor and displacement.

As such, I claim that curricular discourse—as an expression of the unconscious and desire—needs to be approached by listening attentively to the whispers of what is really desired behind the melodic composition of metonymic discursive arrangements.

Britzman (2010) sticks by Freud in indicating that the drive to know is affected by the ego (self-preservation) and the sexual instinct, reason why educational experience is "animated by things that are not biological", nor purely intellectual, but as complex as "love, hate and ambivalence" (p. 33). Since curriculum—as the communicative act that it is—always carries unconscious demands, its psychoanalytic critique establishes a conversation with it asking, as Lacan did: "*Che vous?*", or What do you want?, and the subsequent question that elicits the dialectic demand that curriculum extends to us: What do you want from me?

Such form of critique requires guiding conceptual elements that are sensitive to the fundamental aspects that define the character of curriculum and that represent at the same time the deep cutting questions of psychoanalysis that can help us surface the desire and unconscious material articulated in discourse. Directed at answering the questions of "What are the assumptions embedded in this discourse"? and "What is this trying to accomplish?", at this stage I propose focusing on three elements that bring together fundamental concerns for both curricular and psychoanalytic practice: the conceptualization of the subject, the notion of symptom, and the problem of desire.

Before elaborating on these elements, a few words need to be said about the character of a particularly psychoanalytic form of criticism, in terms of its attitude and problematics.

In his 1993 book on psychoanalytic cultural criticism, Mark Bracher frames his discussion of criticism using as a starting point a rather uncomfortable assessment of the state of field: that the knowledge in the humanities—particularly that from approaches to criticism such as formalism, new historicism, epistemology, among others—has become less relevant to the lives of the people involved in it and for the public at large. His charge is that, historically, only rarely have critics pursued the question of what effects cultural artifacts may have on those who engage with them, and by avoiding issues that may have any subjective significance, they have made "little discernible difference, directly or indirectly, in the lives of most people" (p. 1). Although not speaking from a psychoanalytic perspective, renowned critic George Steiner seems to agree with the assessment, as he deems criticism in isolation from historical, social and biographical contexts "didactically ingenious, but essentially false" (1984, p. 8).

Proposing a shift in the knowledge pursued by critics towards a focus on "how various texts and discourses affect those who use them" (p. ix), Bracher turns to Lacanian psychoanalytic theory, as it provides "one the most effective conceptual apparatuses available for promoting benign social change...through the discourse of cultural criticism" (p. x).

Interest in the subjective effects of cultural artifacts, language, and discourse, their modes of production, circulation, and consumption, links to understanding social change, among others aspects, inevitably bring about the political dimension of critical work.

For Bracher, a distinctive aspect of Lacanian psychoanalysis that proves to be powerful for criticism is its account of the "various roles that language and discourse play in the psychic economy and thereby in human affairs in general" as well as its helpfulness in "explaining how linguistic and discursive phenomena affect specific elements of subjectivity and thus *move* people" (p. 12).

British philosopher and queer theorist Jim Dean (2002) also points to the fact that the social rather than individual dimension of human experience that Lacan clarified by reconceiving the unconscious in terms of language, helps the political, and therefore conflictual, nature of the social become more apparent in criticism. This way, and taking a demystifying stance, cultural criticism—Dean asserts—becomes a form of political work. "The politically progressive critic", he writes, "is always about the business of unmasking, attempting to unveil the ideological struggles behind seemingly innocent or harmonious work....". And specifies that contemporary psychoanalytic criticism "demystifies the transindividual struggles (whether social or ideological) that the work...is understood to encode" (p. 29).

Bracher seems to agree with this political stance, in what appears to be a therapeutic approach, as he insists in linking analysis to the conditions to bring about "benign social change", and invoking other authors that endorse psychoanalytic criticism in terms that it "reconceives texts not only as, in deconstructionist terms, undecidable objects, nor as, in variants of Marxist criticism, ideological templates, but also as sites of effective action, as scenes of forceful statements with consequences..." (1993, p. 23).

Dean, in analyzing the work of Slavoj Zizek (who somehow articulates Lacan and Marxism), seems uncomfortable when confronted with some of the emancipatory insights of psychoanalytic critique that face the therapeutic project with difficult facts: "when Zizek characterizes the ideological field as constituted around a deadlock [i.e. impossibility] that by definition does not admit of discursive or practical manipulation, the possibilities for political struggle and melioration start to seem bleak" (p. 25).

Such preoccupation would perhaps dissipate if we were to shift the question, as Dwayne Huebner once suggested, from how can we control (practical manipulation, or amelioration, in Dean's vocabulary), to how can we see ourselves anew.

In spite of the particularities of Dean's and Bracher's project, they do recognize important elements that characterize the impetus and possibilities of a psychoanalytic approach to criticism. From Dean, that is its engagement in analyzing not only the imaginary and the symbolic representations, but also with that which resists representation: the real, and with it, desire, the drives, and *jouissance*. From Bracher, a form of study that is attentive towards the psycho-social significance and consequences of discourse for the human subjects who encounter and engage with it.

Seen as a problem of reading/interpretation/demystification, psychoanalytic critique is ultimately an issue of transference and countertransference, that is, a matter of the speech act and a confrontation with our desire, resistance", and defenses. As Freud came to realize, it is primarily a matter of listening and speaking and allowing ourselves to be implicated in the conversation. We can see again here an affinity with curricular work when understood as a (complicated) conversation.

A starting point for this conversation that is critique is a phenomenological stance in the sense of the Husserlian dictum of "letting what shows itself be seen for itself", which in psychoanalytic critique means to let the unconscious speak for itself, in the ways it usually speaks: metonymy, metaphor, substitution, and displacement. The attention in this critical conversation can be directed to three aspects that bring together essential foci for understanding the dynamics at play in both analytical and curricular work. Those are the question of the subject, the attention to desire as the element that moves subjectivity and the analytical notion of the symptom as a guide for diagnosis and interpretation of the other two. As such, and in outlining a method of critique, the notions of symptom, desire, and subject become central analytic categories that can help us direct our attention when reading the symptoms in curricular texts.

The Symptom, Desire, and the Subject

The Symptom

As it has been established by psychoanalytic experience, symptoms carry symbolic meaning, and as such—as Lacan noted—are an issue of language. Though presented as metaphors (symptoms, like the unconscious, are structured like a language) they represent "the return of truth" of unconscious content and must, therefore, "be interpreted in the signifying order" (Lacan, *Ècrits*, p. 194). The formation of symptoms can occur from different scenarios. Britzman (2003), for example, focuses on the Freudian account that takes them as the result of a chain preceded by an arousal of danger, an anxiety, a defense and a compromise formation. In this account, symptoms can also be seen as the expression of conflicting desires. But symptoms, like those expressed in physical ailments, can also be triggered not by issues of desire per se, but by a lack of transference of libidinal energy and its fixation in the body (as in those produced in narcissism or hysteria) or by not releasing internal conflicts by use of the word (the symptom as a word trapped in the body. Recall here Lacan's treatment of a woman with abasia, who could not walk without assistance, whose symptom disappeared as soon as her perception of lack of support from her father was exposed).

Interestingly enough, even though a symptom is a pathological formation, it sometimes appears and persists because it provides an unconscious sense of enjoyment (*jouissance*). In Dean's account, in Freudian terms, the symptom "provides an unconscious wish with a surrogate satisfaction" (2002, p. 28). Following Dean, by virtue of defining the symptom semiotically, Lacan initiated a process of universalization of the symptom. In this process, Dean explains, the symptom becomes "a condition of subjective existence rather than a contingent problem" (p. 22). Hence, the focus in analysis is not on the symptom per se to cure it or make it disappear, but on reading it in terms of what is signaling. Considering symptoms as a condition of subjective existence could imply several important aspects. One is that it diminishes the negative pathological weight is carries in the traditional medical perspective. A representation of this is the fact that Lacan does not dichotomize between "normal" and "abnormal". Another aspect is that, as a universalized phenomenon, it allows for the investigation and analysis of symptoms outside of the body, and in the intersubjective expressions of subjects in culture. This is precisely what Zizek does in his work.

As Dean notes, "by shifting symptoms from the category of the exception to that of the rule, Zizek to some extent depathologizes the symptom, converting it into a subjective norm". This universalizing of symptomatology, he adds, "fuels the motive for diagnosis and interpretation, since symptoms are no longer localized and self-evident but lurking everywhere". In this sense, and in the hermeneutic task of analysis and criticism, once one has grasped the structural logic of the symptom "one may submit practically anything of interest to its explanatory grid" (p. 22).

A third aspect is that, as any phenomenon of subjectivity, it does not operate in the same form for everybody and cannot be predicted in their appearance, origin, form or duration. From this perspective, and brought to the field of education, we can see more clearly how curriculum may work as unfinished symptoms, a provocation for the other to respond to the interpellation and thus complete the symptom.

The Subject

The communicative situation that curriculum configures and rests upon, reveals its performative effects in that, in the discursive device of assertion and reiteration, it "produce[s] the phenomena that it regulates and constrains" (Butler 1993, p. xii). One such phenomena is the restructuration of subjectivity. Anne Phelan (2015) invokes Hanna Arendt to explain that in the assembly of people not only ideas or approaches are debated and exchanged, but rather is a "space of appearance in which individuals and groups appear to one another, in the process of creating their subjectivities" (Benhabib 2008, in Phelan 2015, p. 3). As part of an ongoing process, subjectivity is, as Phelan notes, "an event rather than a project of completion", one where the subject is continuously in "a state of becoming" (p. 3).

The process of becoming that Phelan is alluding to is never straightforward. For one, the curricular event is, by definition, a site of struggle of different and sometimes opposing intentionalities. This is highlighted by Deborah Britzman (2014) when she cites Mikael Bakhtin (1981) in his assertion that the communicative situation—such as the curriculum situation—is "populated – overpopulated- with the intentions of others" (pp. 321–322). These intentions, which are enacted in the speech act, have performative consequences beyond their mere expression. As Taubman strongly asserts, "our sexuality, our so-called inner being, our deepest emotions, our most heartfelt interests…are shaped by and in language" (2011, p. 172). As such, we can think of curriculum as not only implicated in but as structurant of the subject, as it is a space that brings together intentions that are not only exercised systematically and sustained in time, but also policed and evaluated. But the problem of understanding the notion of subject is complex and demands an exploration of at least three elements that can help explain its constitution.

The Mirror Stage

One aspect that is fundamental in the work of Jacques Lacan and that helps in understanding the process of subjection is what he termed the mirror stage, as it explores the conditions for the very beginning of the production of subjectivity and its subsequent development. In general terms, this stage[1] starts in the final phase of weaning, and its marked by the individual's capacity for representation—that is—the entrance into the symbolic. When the baby first recognizes that the image he/she sees in the mirror is, precisely that, an image outside of him/herself, the representation of the image begins to have a powerful impression on the ego, and the construction of the idea we have about ourselves.

---

[1] It is worth noting here that even though the mirror stage first appears linked to a particular point of developmental maturity, the term stage in Lacan is not tied to the developmental discourse of psychology or the natural sciences, but rather it refers to the presence of a moment marked by a before and after.

In "The family complexes in the formation of the individual" (first published in French in 1938), Lacan makes a short statement with important implications. He notes that "before the ego affirms its own identity it confuses itself with this image which forms it, but also subjects it to a primordial alienation" (p. 32). This primordial alienation will constitute one of the most significant traits of the subject for Lacan: the fact that, contrary to the illusion of the subject as a unitary self in psychology, the subject is divided, split. The moment of weaning marks the primordial drama for the human being: the separation from the breast of the mother, and henceforth, the destruction of the oceanic feeling of oneness. This is the moment of the appearance of the other that is not me. The implications are manifold, but an important one for our discussion is that the mirror stage marks the emergence of desire hand in hand with the entering into the realm of language.

As Peter Taubman (2011) explains it, "…in severing us from the fantasized paradisiacal maternal oneness – fantasized because it was always torn by loss and rage as well as ecstasy – the symbolic marks the beginning of desire, desire to be whatever it is we imagine the M(o)ther desires, so we can regain that oneness". As he further explains, because "we never achieve this fantasized bliss of pre-Oedipal union, we wind up looking for the answer to the question and the lost oneness in all sorts of substitutions, which we demand" (p. 167). As such, the mirror stage inaugurates a double process that continues to operate throughout our lifetime: the tendency to invest our subjectivity on images (at the level of the ego), and the ongoing pursuit for the satisfaction of desires.

Analytically then, behind every utterance and symptomatic expression, we might ask what is the desire that expression is concealing.

As it provides important antecedents not only to the emergence of the subject but to that of desire (and the ongoing search and demand into which it throws us) the mirror stage is a key aspect in the exploration of the subject.

Language and Temporality

When Lacan locates the subject in the symbolic order, distinguishing it from the ego (which he locates in the imaginary) he sets in motion important consequences for the understanding and investigation of subjectivity, not only for the practice of analysis in the context of psychotherapy but also for education and the critique of curriculum.

One of them, that although may sound basic and commonsensical, is one that points to the very central nature of both the analytical and pedagogical act: their enactment and reconstructive power through the use of language. Pedagogy, as psychoanalysis, is an intervention in the real by means of the symbolic, which is a central aspect that set these practices apart from others such as psychology or pharmacology.

This intervention not only has creative effects (as in its performative effect of producing that which it names) and therapeutic effects (as in the ability to drive inner conflicts out by transferring them through words) but also has a function of recognition of ourselves and the other. This is to a great extent to what Taubman refers when he says that it is in language that our inner beings, our most heartfelt interests, and sexuality are shaped. To this Britzman (2014) adds that the pedagogical exchange is also affected by the erotic undercurrents of communication.

The pedagogical encounter, as the analytical one, Britzman (2003) explains, is marked by anxiety. This is because—as Anna Freud notes—"words arouse anxiety" (in Britzman 2003, p. 83). This is one of the aspects in which the communicative nature of the pedagogical encounter reveals itself as a phenomenon mediated by temporality. Following Anna Freud, Britzman explains that anxiety is "the special way for the ego to anticipate what might happen next" (p. 87). As such, curricular discourse occupies a complex and always sliding positioning in temporality, drawing from the past to make the present intelligible, while tending to what might happen in the future. In Education then, "events both actual and imagined are forcibly felt before they can be known" (Britzman 2003, p. 7) making "learning" and understanding—like the symptom—something that can only be recognized in retrospective.

"If we have learned anything from psychoanalysis", James Macdonald (in Pinar 1975) maintains, "is that the past dwells in the present" (p. 15), but the presence of anxiety reminds us that another dweller in the present is the future. In this constant flow of temporality, critique might be thought of as a momentary anchoring point that stops the otherwise endless sliding of signification.

In considering the temporal dimension of curriculum—which is inextricably mediated by biography—one is reminded of the reflections of Hermann Hesse's young Brahmin Siddhartha, while he was sitting on a riverbank: "*It strikes him that once the measurement of time is waived, the past and the future are ever-present, like the river, which at one and the same moment exists not only where he sees it to be, but also at its source and its mouth. The water which has yet to pass is tomorrow, but it already exists upstream; and that which has passed is yesterday, but it still exists, elsewhere downstream*" (Terziani 2002). This way, and as in Carolyn Dinshaw's (2012) discussion of the meaning of "now", it can be said that the curricular situation—in its temporal and biographical dimension—is a permanent state of transition: the overlap of the "already" and "not yet". Unlike the modern (and neoliberal) view of temporality, which is linear, measurable and oriented to the future, the analytic stance shows that the past conditions our experience of the present in powerful ways, though it can in no way determine our futures in predictable ways. In a piece titled "Curriculum as concern for man's temporality" (originally published in 1967), Dwayne Huebner points out that the orientation to the future embedded in the language of "goals" and "objectives" basically obliterate a basic awareness of historicity. One of the problems of such lack of awareness of the past is that it blinds us to what has been our own complicity with what we are experiencing in the perceived present and leaves us trapped in the compulsion to act by repetition.

In the juncture of language and temporality though, there is another and often ignored phenomenon that brings together language, desire, and unconscious in the formation of the subject: that of the enigmatic signifier.

The Enigmatic Signifier

In explaining the constitution of the subject in the inextricable relationship of desire and language (thus, establishing the notion of the subject as *parlêtre*, a speaking being), Jacques Lacan developed an illustration of the process which came to be known as the Graph of Desire (Fig. 3.1).

Risking oversimplification, a really brief and basic way to read the graph would go like this. We start from the delta on the lower right hand of the graph. The delta represents a need (which can be bodily, affective, or otherwise). The need passes through C, which stands for code (the code of language) and it then turns into a message (represented in M). The message is always first sanctioned by the code. The horizontal dotted line that moves from left to right has to do with synchrony and the history of language and its resources, that which precedes us as subjects, marking the laws of the code and the intelligibility of the message. This

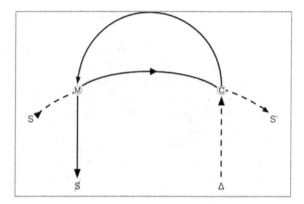

Fig. 3.1 Graph of desire

history of language, in moving against the subject, would help explain why we sometimes say what we did not mean to say. The last element in this version of the graph—the barred S—is the result of the process: the split subject.

This is the model by which Lacan also illustrates the "anchoring point", or the way in which the signifier "hooks" or stops the otherwise endless sliding of signification, thus demonstrating that meaning is something that can only be seen in retrospect[2] (notice the arrow moving backward from need towards the subject), subverting the Sausserian model that gave primacy to the signified.

So far, the process that produces the subject in direct relation to the signifier seems somewhat transparent and straightforward, but it's far from that. One key problem—for the context of this discussion—is that the code can never fully absorb all of the need. Perhaps a too simplistic but quotidian example from everyday life that helps in illustrating the point is the fact that when one bangs a finger with a hammer and says "ouch" (or whatever it is one says on such situation) the language used cannot really and fully contain or represent what we are experiencing. There is a portion of life—need and suffering—that remains unspoken, unspeakable, undecidable.

---

[2]On this issue, Joël Dor (1997) notes that "a sign can make sense only retroactively, since the signification of a message emerges only at the end of the signifying utterance itself" (p. 41).

In acknowledging the presence and effect of "that which resists representation", Lacan brings to the fore the dimension of the Real and its associated elements of what remains in the unconscious, such as the drives, *jouissance* and the *objet petit a*, or the unattainable object of desire.

As Jim Dean explains in his piece Art as Symptom (2002), contrary to the Anglo-American misunderstanding of Lacan's theory as deterministic and as revoking subjective agency for insisting in the constitutive effect of the symbolic (the signifier), he actually emphasized the "*under-*determination of subjectivity by symbolic forms". This is so since these forms "can never completely determine subjective effects" because "there is always something left over, something unexplained by symbolic determination" (p. 24). This leftover is what brings in the notion of the enigmatic signifier.

Quoting from Lacan's piece "The instance of the letter in the unconscious" (Ècrits), Dean focuses his attention on a passage where Lacan refers more directly to the notion of enigmatic signifier and the way it operates: "between the enigmatic signifier…and the term that is substituted for it in an actual signifying chain there passes the spark that fixes in a symptom the signification inaccessible to the conscious subject…a symptom being a metaphor in which flesh or function is taken as a signifying element" (p. 34).

In other words, and considering the graph of desire we saw previously, the enigmatic signifier is something that comes out of the delta of the unconscious (a need, a conflict, suffering) but instead of appearing transparently as what it is, it substitutes itself for another term in the signifying chain of language. As such, Dean asserts, the enigmatic signifier "does not form part of a signifying chain but instead causes something else to take its place; the enigmatic signifier, therefore, isn't a signifier in any general acceptance of the term" (p. 34).

Even though it gets fixed in a symptom, the content of the enigmatic signifier stems from the unconscious Real and remains inaccessible to consciousness.

But in understanding curriculum as an unfinished symptom, the presence and performative consequences of the enigmatic signifier are not limited to "what is not said" (as in hidden curriculum) but in reality to any enunciated utterance or gesture. As such, the symptomatology triggered by the curricular situation, driven by the enigmatic signifier, becomes universalized and, by extension, to a great extent depathologized.

Since the enigmatic signifier "remains enigmatic because it remains unconscious" (Dean 2002, p. 35), it poses a heuristic and analytical challenge for the practice of interpretation and critique.

It appears that it does not operate by making itself readily interpretable or readable, but rather by means of seduction. Of allowing glimpses of the desires it manifests in assertions, demands, metaphors, symbolisms, metonymies, and slips of the tongue and pen.

The enigmatic signifier epitomizes the complexity of a psychoanalytic approach to critique of curriculum: instead of pretending to gather and build up meaning (as in classic hermeneutics) the methodological technique would consist more in what Dean describes as "interpretation stripped down to pointing—a kind of pointing that works to punctuate the subject's discourse, cutting it into its discrete components" (p. 36). Positioned from an appreciation for the Freudian technique of free association, this "pointing" as an interpretive investigative approach is elaborated by Laplanche, who describes it this way: "...*The German deuten, Deutung, is here much more eloquent, and much less "hermeneutic" than our word "interpretation":* deuten auf *means to indicate with a finger or with the eyes – "to point", as the Lacanians would say*" (cited in Dean 2002, p. 36). Methodologically, this reminds of Pinar's approach based on juxtaposed commentary.

Desire

Reading cultural expressions as symptoms involves recognizing the trajectory and direction of desire. Desire longs for recognition and acknowledgment, that is why it expresses itself through the appearance of symptoms. As a propelling force of human existence and agency, desire occupies a prominent place of attention for psychoanalytic theory and practice. An important part of what we say, feel, think, do or try to do (and sometimes what we fail to say or do) is predicated on desire. Although desire can sometimes appear to be very similar to need and demand, they are not exactly the same thing. A need remains linked to biologic functions and instincts, and demands are the linguistic expression of such needs. While the articulation of a need in a demand can usually satisfy the need until a new one arises, demand cannot really satisfy—if only temporarily—another basic human craving: the love of the Other.

Here is where desire appears and is revealed in its complex nature. As Dylan Evans (1996) puts it, while "the Other can provide the objects which the subject requires to satisfy his needs, the Other cannot provide that unconditional love which the subject craves. Hence even after the needs which were articulated in demand have been satisfied, the other aspect of demand, the craving for love, remains unsatisfied, and this leftover is desire". Paraphrasing Lacan, Evans attempts a definition: "Desire is…the surplus produced by the articulation of need in demand" (p. 38). Desire, then, is not about reaching satisfaction necessarily, but about the ongoing reproduction of desire, of continuing wanting to be loved by the Other, to desire and be desired. Desire, as a mobilizing force, keeps us going and recognizing the other as we seek to be recognized by them.

It is desire what explains the act of "appearing to one another" in the process of production of subjectivity in which Anne Phelan framed her discussion of education we mentioned earlier, and what underlies all ethics of care.

As a subtle, unconscious, yet powerful element in the configuration and (re)construction of subjectivity, a psychoanalytic critique of curriculum should address in one way or another the desire(s) that might be played out (both in explicit expressions and in the subtler appearances through the enigmatic signifier) in the discourse that regulates and organizes the formation of people.

As Bracher (1993) points out, "insofar as a cultural phenomenon succeeds in interpellating subjects – that is, summoning them to assume a certain subjective (dis)position", just as curriculum does, "it does so by evoking some form of desire or by promising satisfaction of some desire". He then poses the centrality of desire with confident conviction: "It is thus desire rather than knowledge that must become the focal point of cultural criticism if we are to understand how cultural phenomena move people" (p. 19).

In popular culture, the concept of desire is often connected with sexuality. Although desire has libidinal ties, it is not always directed to a sexual object, but it is, in fact, sexual in nature. Citing Lacan, Evans points out that "Unconscious desire is entirely sexual; the motives of the unconscious are limited…to sexual desire" (p. 37).

Establishing relations with other people, appearing to one another, seeking their gaze, seducing them to assume a certain subject position (or forcing them to, as its often the case in education) are expressions of desire sustained in libidinal ties.

Perhaps such sexual motive of desire is more evidently embodied in the pedagogical enactment of those of queer identity, as is the potentially therapeutic effect of a practice that supports such expression of subjectivity. Peter Taubman (2011) shows how, as recorded in the minutes of the Vienna Psychoanalytic Society in 1910, Sigmund Freud expressed that "problems in education" were "connected with the growing proscription of homosexuality" at the time, because "in suppressing the practice of homosexuality, one has simply suppressed the homosexual direction of human feeling that is so necessary for our society". Further, Freud added that "the best teachers are the real homosexuals" (p. 4). Intriguing as such statements might be, libidinal ties—regardless of sexual orientation—are the driving force for human interaction, yet their acknowledgment continues to cause discomfort and be regarded as problematic, particularly in the pedagogical situation. When it comes to desire, the truth of the matter is that someone wants something, wants something for him/her, and from the other.

Deborah Britzman (2014) argues that we do know that education wants something from the teacher, and for that matter, we could affirm that public policy in particular certainly wants something from those who are to become teachers or other professionals. But she also reverses the question, recasting the psychoanalytic questions that Anna Freud once asked: what does the teacher want for herself/himself? It is then, when confronted with one's own, that the issue of desire proves to be even more uncomfortable: "typically", Britzman writes, "the teacher's persona may present itself as altruistic, self-effacing and idealistic. Rarely are these character masks considered as defences against the fear of autobiography and the chaos of desire" (p. 124).

WHAT ARE THE IMPLICATIONS OF A PSYCHOANALYTIC CRITIQUE OF CURRICULUM?

Psychoanalysis is far from being popular or fashionable, at least in the traditional academic establishment. As Peter Taubman (2011) shows, the history of the relationship between psychoanalysis and education has been a problematic, even a "neurotic" one. Particularly in North America, Taubman explains, psychoanalysis has been the object of rejection and disavowal (or actually, resistance), in part, due to its disturbing knowledge and disinterest with pragmatic translations of its insights. "Its absence", Taubman asserts, "is particularly glaring in teacher education and in educational policy, where the learning sciences, neoliberal agendas, and business models determine the dominant approaches to education and provide the terms to describe teaching and curriculum" (pp. 1–2). Psychoanalytic theories, which work "on the border between the socio/cultural and the intrapsychic" are ignored or disparaged, even when they help "explore the mysteries of subjectivity and… can illuminate the dreams, desires, ideals, and terrors that shape our understanding of education" (p. 2). Although the implications of a psychoanalytic reading of curricular discourse are manifold, here I would like to mention three of them, as they relate more specifically with the process of subjection in the context of teacher education.

First, the psychoanalytic understanding of language—and the role of the Signifier in relation to the signified in particular—actually constitute a theory of the subject. As such, it is central to the discussion of curricular work. As Manuel Asensi has pointed out,[3] when Ferdinand de Saussure elaborates what became the basis of modern semiotics, organized in the formula of signified/signifier, and tied it to psychology, he was actually articulating the classic notion of the subject (one that operates by conscious control) which is the underlying notion that operates in much of modern social sciences. By subverting it, and placing the Signifier above the signified in the formula, Lacan redefines the theory of the subject, giving way to the recognition of the unconscious and its understanding as a language phenomenon.

For the context of curriculum studies, taking this redefinition seriously implies an ongoing retheorizing of curriculum as text[4]: a racial, gendered, class, temporal and spatial text (see Pinar 1975, 1995, 2006, 2015). Understood from a psychoanalytic vantage point, curriculum then appears as a human arrangement that inscribes subjectivity by posing unfinished symptoms that elicit completion in diverse ways. As such, and by virtue of exerting preset meanings, and imposing delimitations, it also opens up and inaugurates the possibility for individuals to assert themselves in their own subjective terms, reinvigorating the ongoing reconstruction of subjectivity, the quest of desire, and ultimately, the re-invention of freedom.

---

[3] In his series of talks "Lacan para multitudes", offered at the Museum of Contemporary Art of Barcelona in 2014.

[4] Referring to the textuality of practices, Derrida asserted that: "every social practice passes through texts and every text is in itself a social practice" (dialogue recorded by Revista Zona Erógena, N° 35, 1997).

Second, criticism is ultimately an act of countertransference on the part of the curriculum worker. Predicated on the notion that curriculum is structured in language, the act of criticism works, as in analysis, as a form of attentive listening, an engagement with the text, or psychoanalytic narrative of the free flow of discourse. This attentive analytic listening does not consider all of what is expressed, though. As both Freud and Lacan suggest, analytic listening pays attention to particular utterances, sometimes even a single word, as they might convey more productive elements that express the unconscious material of their origin.

In this sense, while the relationship that the analysand/student/text establishes with the analyst/curriculum scholar is one based on transference, I suggest that the act of curricular criticism finds its efficacy on the countertransference. That is, a capture of that which the text is expressing in terms of the particular ways in which the critic listens: a filter that continuously asks, "where is this coming from"? "what do you want?", "what do you want from me?".

It is an inquisitive listening that, informed by academic knowledge and animated by conviction, relies on judgment to fix attention on one or other utterance, discerning what might be the enigmatic signifier(s) that were replaced in the actual chain of signification of curricular discourse.

Third, an understanding that the purpose of psychoanalysis is not to make us feel better, or "produce" or ameliorate anything, but to allow us to be ourselves more authentically. As Argentinian psychoanalyst Marie Langer would put it, psychoanalysis is useful to better understand ourselves and to try to stop lying to ourselves.

Psychoanalytic critique, though disavowed or disparaged for bringing up uncomfortable knowledge, might be precisely what is needed in such a time as this. In the context of higher education, Matthew Clarke and Anne Phelan (2015) denounce a surplus of positivity, particularly in teacher education, which is marked by an anxious reliance on standards, recipes for action, and the therapeutic ego-stroking practice of back patting. However, the virtue of negativity, they point out, is its ability to unsettle and disrupt the comfortable stance of the "given" order of things. It could be said that it is the often uncomfortable knowledge of the understanding of self and the other that gets us in a position to be willing for subjective reconstruction and change.

It is in analysis, after all, Lacan pointed out, that we are allowed to fully acknowledge what has been our own history.

REFERENCES

Bennett, A. (2004). *The History Boys*. London: Faber and Faber Limited.
Bracher, M. (1993). *Lacan, Discourse and Social Change: A Psychoanalytic Cultural Criticism*. Ithaca and London: Cornell University Press.
Britzman, D. (2003). *After-Education: Anna Freud, Melanie Klein, and Psychoanalytic Histories of Learning*. Albany: SUNY Press.
Britzman, D. (2009). *The Very Thought of Education: Psychoanalysis and the Impossible Professions*. Albany, NY: SUNY Press.
Britzman, D. (2010). *Freud and Education*. New York: Routledge.
Britzman, D. (2014). That Other Scene of Pedagogy: A Psychoanalytic Narrative. *Changing English*, 21(2), 122–130.
Butler, J. (1993). *Bodies That Matter: On the Discursive Limits of "Sex"*. New York: Routledge.
Clarke, M., & Phelan, A. (2015) The Power of Negative Thinking in and for Teacher Education. *Power & Education* 0(0), pp. 1–15.
Dean, J. (2002). Art as Symptom: Zizek and the Ethics of Psychoanalytic Criticism. *Diacritics*, 32(2), 21–41.
Dinshaw, C. (2012). *How Soon Is Now? Medieval Texts, Amateur Readers, and the Queerness of Time*. Durham and London: Duke University Press.
Doll, W. (2015). Seeking a Method Beyond Method. Keynote presented at the fifth triennial conference of the International Association for the Advancement of Curriculum Studies, University of Ottawa.
Dor, J. (1997). *Introduction to the Reading of Lacan: The Unconscious Structured Like a Language*. New York: Rowman & Littlefield.
Evans, D. (1996). *An Introductory Dictionary of Lacanian Psychoanalysis*. London: Routledge.
Foucault, M. (1997). *The Politics of Truth*. South Pasadena, CA: Semiotext(e).
Habermas, J. (1972). *Knowledge and Human Interests*. Beacon Press.
Horkheimer, M. (2000). *Teoría Tradicional y Teoría Crítica*. España: Paidós.
Lacan, J. (1989). *The Family Complexes*. London: W. W. Norton.
Phelan, A. (2015). *Curriculum Theorizing and Teacher Education: Complicating Conjunctions*. Routledge.
Pinar, W. (1975). *Curriculum Theorizing: The Reconceptualists*. Berkeley: Mccutchan Pub Corp.
Pinar, W. (1995). *Understanding Curriculum: An Introduction to the Study of Historical and Contemporary Curriculum Discourses*. New York: Peter Lang.
Pinar, W. (2006). *The Synoptic Text Today and Other Essays: Curriculum Development After the Reconceptualization*. New York: Peter Lang.
Pinar, W. (2015). *Educational Experience as Lived. Knowledge, History, Alterity: The Collected Works of William F. Pinar*. Taylor & Francis.

Ruitenberg, C. (2009). The Question of Method in Philosophy of Education. *Journal of Philosophy of Education*, 43(3), 315–323.
Steiner, G. (1984). *A Reader*. Penguin Books.
Taubman, P. (2011). *Disavowed Knowledge: Psychoanalysis, Education and Teaching*. New York: Routledge.
Terziani, T. (2002). *A Fortune-Teller Told Me: Earthbound Travels in the Far East*. New York: Broadway Books.

CHAPTER 4

Analyzing Symptoms in Policy: A Psychoanalytic Reading

Abstract This chapter offers a Lacanian psychoanalytic critique of the World Bank's global educational policy for curricular reform. Looking at curricular discourse as a symptom, this analysis performs a critical reading of the enunciations of the text identifying their origins and effects in the Lacanian registers of the Real, the Symbolic and the Imaginary. Asking questions such as "What are the conditions that the framing of the policy establish for the emergence of the subject?", this chapter analyzes the interplay of symptom, language, and subject, as expressed in the transference between the discourse and the reader. The chapter closes with a discussion of the psychic consequences of defining education in transactional terms that disavow subjectivity.

Keywords Policy analysis · Curricular reform · Transference Symptoms

INTRODUCTION

An authentic psychoanalytic understanding and investigation of the unconscious, in the tradition inaugurated by Sigmund Freud, is one based on the exploration of the psychic functions of language and the workings of the transference.

In this tradition, one is invited to overthrow received meanings about education and reconceive it in terms of its psychic significance in the (re)construction of the subject. One is invited to ask, for example, in what ways psychoanalytic criticism may affect the ways in which we account for education and, in reality, analyze the very thought of education (Britzman 2010).

Such a question may be timely and precisely what is needed, particularly at a historical moment when the process of formation of professionals in general, and of teachers in particular, is going through a global curricular reform movement of standardization directed by a liaison of political-economic institutions. International agencies such as the World Bank, the Inter American Bank for Development, UNESCO, and Project Tuning (European Union and Latin America) have been actively involved in designing, funding, and directing governments across the globe in the installation and implementation of their educational agenda. In a discourse that reiteratively shrouds in the logics of quality improvement, these agencies recast higher education as a transactional activity, one that can be measured and assessed in the performance of particular competencies, and verified in its use-value in the labor market. Presenting the curriculum as a matter of input–output, standards, protocols, competencies, benchmarks, comparability, transferability, rate of return, employability, and usefulness for the labor market, they redefine higher education as a system of functions of the economic sector.

And the stakes are high: the intervention in structures of psychic dynamics that predispose individuals to think, act and feel in a particular way in relation to themselves and those around them. In other words, it is the very process of subjection what lies at the center of curricular activity. After all, and as Canadian curricular theorist Ted Aoki would point out, those who control the language of a field also control its present and its becoming. Jacoby (1986, cited in Taubman 2011) gives testimony of some of the consequences that happen when changing the language of a discipline to one that is foreign to its orientation and purpose: "the translation of psychoanalysis into a professional and scientific enterprise affected its language, spirit, breadth and even those attracted to it. Fewer and fewer individuals with humanists, intellectual or political commitments entered the discipline" (p. 141).

Several decades before a curricular reform would reach such encompassing discursive and geopolitical magnitude as the one we are experiencing today, William Pinar (1975) had already elaborated an accurate diagnosis of the system of schooling of modernity. The conditions they impose are not only deteriorating for psychic development: they are maddening.

In the context of such widely shared diagnosis—one that stands true today—psychoanalysis operates in the understanding that cure oftentimes requires the recognition of difference. This analytical operation might not be as simple as one might think, particularly in the context of an ever-encompassing push for homogenization (something typical of totalitarian agendas). In the present conditions of rampant neoliberalism,[1] the push for standardization and homogenization has brought with it a reduction of the notion of the subject, and rather, its reification. Although subjectivity and its objectification have been discussed in important ways from a political perspective (see the work of Paulo Freire, for example), a psychoanalytic view allows for a closer look at the dynamics that take place in the process.

It is in this context of growing standardization and presentation of education as a mainly cognitive and logical process that the central notions of psychoanalysis, such as desire, libido, aggressiveness, and other expressions of the unconscious, appear as subversive functions. In the recognition that education and the drive to know are fully invested with libidinal ties and desire, and that the investments of the unconscious cannot be controlled nor predicted, psychoanalysis appears as problematic, unsettling and subversive knowledge. Perhaps, it is precisely what is needed in the exercise of a critique directed at determining the underlying assumptions and psychic structures on which discursive practices rest, in the art of "not being governed so much".

This chapter is a preliminary attempt to perform a Lacanian psychoanalytic reading of the discourse in official documentation from the agencies that are having a direct impact in directing curricular reform across the globe, i.e. the World Bank and Tuning.

Looking at the curricular discourse of this documentation as symptoms, the analysis elaborated here enacts rethinking as a method, a way of "thinking through" the text to discern the symbolizations that create the conditions for the formation of subjectivity. The critical reading of the enunciations of the text is done as a form of listening to the transference in the free discursive flow of the text in regard to the interplay of

---

[1] One wonders whether the term "neoliberal" still applies, given the now universal and unescapable marketization of both private and public life, where truly there is no alternative. Dismissing one of its central pillars, that of freedom of choice, liberalism in its present form is no longer "neo" (a revitalization of its central assumptions), but rather post-liberalism.

symptom, language and subject (in curricular terms, as sketched in the previous chapter), while attempting to identify their dynamics and effects in the Lacanian registers of the Real, the Symbolic and the Imaginary.

In the effort to understand the symbolizations of internal plurality (Britzman 2009) and the fundamental factors that are operative in what conditions educational experience (Pinar 1975) this piece is animated by the question "*che vous?*", exploring questions such as "What are the conditions that the framing of curricular policy establishes for the emergence of the subject?"; "What are the symptoms expressed in the text?"; and "What are the (unfinished) symptoms it elicits for completion by the other?".

About Tuning and the World Bank

The current scenario of global curricular reform of higher education is composed of various actors, but two agencies are key to understanding the process due to the extent of their influence and their practical impact on both the design of policies and practices and the funding for governments to adopt them. One is Tuning (European Union and Tuning Latin America) and the other is the World Bank and its "Task Force on Higher Education and Society".

The discourse and practices of both agencies find antecedents in the Jomtien Declaration (1990) and the Bologna Process (started in 1999), where the notion of education as tied to rate-of-return analysis was first powerfully installed in the international community (in the former) and the idea of securing quality via comparability across systems of higher education in connection to the labor market (in the latter).

Tuning is a European organization based at the University of Deusto, Spain, created as a practical way to implement the agreements signed in the Bologna Process, linking political demands with higher education. It is defined as an approach to "(re)design, develop, implement and evaluate study programmes" (Gonzáles and Wagenaar 2008, p. 9). The approach sustained on the overall framework of competency-based curriculum, is presented as a process primarily focused on educational structures (subject areas within institutions) rather than educational systems (governments level). However, the influence of the approach is now not only present in the countries of the European Union, but also in America (Francophone Canada and Latin American countries) through the creation of Tuning Latin America. Thus, Tuning declares that it "can be considered valid worldwide" (p. 9).

The World Bank, on the other hand, in its key document "Peril and Promise" (2000)—developed by their "Task Force for Higher Education and Society"—does declare a focus on educational systems across the globe, having as primary audience government officials, higher education policymakers, and anyone in a decision-making position "responsible for enacting reforms" (p. 20). The document does three things: (a) it defines the role of higher education in supporting the process of economic development (b) identifies the obstacles in higher education for that aim, and (c) it sketches solutions to overcome such obstacles.

Although it declares not to be a "universal blueprint for reforming higher education systems" (p. 14), their warning of "the cost of being left behind" and "having to face a future of increasing exclusion" (pp. 14–15), their recommendations on funding models, governance and curriculum development expressed as "the bottom line", and the monetary funding they provide for the implementation of such policies suggest otherwise.

Due to the encompassing influence of this document in particular, both in the definition of the international political agenda for higher education reform, and its framing of a notion of knowledge, professionals, and their purpose and processes of formation—central elements of attention for curriculum—the analysis presented here focuses its attention on this particular text.

THE SYMPTOMS IN WORLD BANK'S "PERIL AND PROMISE" (2000)

Fear and the Discourse of the Master

One of the first elements that stand out from the signifying chain of the discourse of the "Task Force" put together by the World Bank, is the conditions it uses to sustain its interpellation. From the title of the document onwards, the discourse of higher education global reform it constructs is predicated on the use of the interpellative force of fear.

In a linguistic strategy not uncommon in political speech, the text frames its presentation in a recursive allusion to a present situation of crisis and a foreboding menace of disastrous consequences if the conditions set as the solution are not followed.

Instances of this framing are found from the very opening and throughout the text. Before developing its agenda for the improvement of "quality", the text declares:

> "*...higher education is in a perilous state*" (p. 16); "*...without better higher education...countries will find it increasingly difficult to benefit from global economy*" (p. 9). But along with sketching the dire consequences that connect the institutions of higher education with the fate of their countries: "*...without improved human capital...countries will fall behind and experience marginalization and isolation...the result will be rising poverty*" (p. 18), it also poses a more dramatic scenario for the whole of society: "*...societies [will be] dangerously unprepared for survival in tomorrow's world*" (p. 16). Using medical/hygienic terms, it asseverates that "*...misery has become an infectious disease*" (p. 20).

Following Bracher's (1993) criticism of political speech, we find here that the force that sustains this framing derives from the insistent imposition of what Lacan called master signifiers, or the arbitrary attempt to universalize a variance of meanings into a unity.

Constructed on the dialectic of peril and promise (threat and solution), the discourse of the World Bank is positioned as the discourse of the master, which is instantiated in the repetitive enunciation of what governments "need to do", the definition of "core qualities", the type of knowledge that is "critical" in today's economy, the "starting points" for action and the "bottom line" of the matter. As such, they are constituted as master signifiers that set the terms of the situation and predefine the roles of that who sets the Law, and those who need to heed its demand.

The master signifiers that define what is "critical", "urgent" and the "core qualities" for today's higher education are also appropriately enunciated in the tone of the text, which although presented as a suggestion, it defines what "must" be done and "implemented" by governments, or dire consequences will follow. The report proceeds by "reasoned argument, relying heavily on experience and belief" (p. 21), but the audience of the text is not invited to discuss the terms of such arguments. As the report declares, their key audiences such as policymakers and higher education professionals "who are responsible for *enacting* reforms" (my italics), are summoned to "translate" the terms of the demands "into new ways of working" (p. 21). Of the general public, like students, it requests "their understanding", as it is "necessary" for the process to run.

Imaginary Threat

The efficacy of the interpellation of such master signifiers and tone can be partially explained in the ambivalence of its appeal: on the one hand, it hinges on fear. The perception of threat and the feeling of fear can have both an immobilizing effect as well as they can be a prompt for rapid action. The use of foreboding images as that of "rising poverty", "isolation", "unpreparedness for survival", among others, play powerfully at the level of the ego. In Freud's account of the psychical apparatus, the ego has as the main function the mediation with the outside world, working primarily in terms of self-preservation and the avoidance of unpleasure. As such, the "perils" to which the text constantly refer are a powerful and direct appeal to the ego and one of its primordial functions.

Following Bracher (1993), the sense of threat "affects one's narcissistic sense of security not only at the symbolic level"—something the text accomplishes by the strategy of reiteration—"but also in the Imaginary register". As such, words selected by the World Bank's Task Force, like the ones just mentioned, work with a "subtle but ominous resonance for the body ego that is at the core of our narcissism and sense of well-being" (pp. 121–122).

On the other hand, the master signifiers and tone also appeal to the activation of an image or ego-ideal of moral obligation. Perhaps tapping on a sense of heroism, the definition of "solutions" presented as "promise" activate a practical stance on the audience, making them susceptible to comply and do what it takes to install conditions that, unpopular as they may be, are deemed rational and aimed for the greater good, to spare the nation of rising difficulties as presented by the world's most influential financial institution.

Specular Constructions in the Imaginary

As we can see, the threat is imaginary. Part of the solution suggested by the World Bank, in its urge to act and "waste no time" (p. 97), is also predicated on imaginary constructions.

In sketching the characteristics of higher education (the social institution it seeks to reform), the World Bank presents it in this way:

> "Higher education is expected to embody norms of social interaction such as open debate and argumentative reason; to emphasize the autonomy and self-reliance of its individual members; and to reject discrimination...".

> The best higher education institution is a model and an impetus for creating a modern civil society. This is an ideal that is not often realized, but is nevertheless a standard against which to measure national systems. (p. 44)

What we see here is that the whole idea of higher education is constructed on an image, an ideal of what is expected. It installs an *imagos* of an institution that embodies social norms, that is a model for civil society. Paradoxically, the World Bank acknowledges the inexistence of such institution in reality (*"an ideal that is not often realized"*), yet it assumes it as "the standard against which to measure national systems".

Not only the standard of the institution it uses to judge the system is imaginary. The subjects it educates are also constructed in the same register: "*...higher education helps to promote the enlightened citizens who are necessary for a democracy*" (p. 44). Yet the image is left up for the reader to complete on her own terms, as the text makes no elaboration around what an "enlightened citizen" might be. The problem is not a matter of more or less detailed descriptions of the image though.

The problem with the reliance on the register of the imaginary for subjective formation is twofold: first, images are extremely precarious. They break. They cannot, therefore, sustain our notions of value or dignity, at least not for long. The second one is that privileging the strengthening of the ego (located in the register of the imaginary) also strengthens one of its central features: that of adaptation to reality (something ego psychology profits enormously from). One can start thinking about the political implications of such a developed attitude of compliance and social adaptation.

As a psychic dynamic, Jacques Lacan did not hold back in his attack against the psychological practice of imaginary strengthening of the (conscious) ego, as it is from there that enslaving suffering stems. This is why, in the opening quotation, Lacan sees in the severing of the knot of imaginary servitude an act of love.

Aggressiveness

The imposition of an image after which higher education, the people who work in it, and the future professionals must conform to is an act of aggressiveness. This is so not just because of the arbitrariness of the World Bank's curricular policy or the imposition of its enforcement through monetary incentives for governments. For Lacan, aggressiveness is always already embedded in language as, by virtue of speaking, we impose meaning on the other.

Though we tend to think of aggressiveness in negative terms, as something undesirable that needs to be removed, I would like to suggest that the presence of an imposed image might be precisely what ignites the (creative) educational work to occur.

Aggressiveness—which for Lacan is central to the formation of the I—requires the presence of a Gestalt, an image against which we construct a notion of unity about ourselves. It is only then that the image can be destroyed—shattered—opening space for self-assertion, and the emergence of the subjective self in its own terms. This operation cannot be done replacing one image with another image (as psychology does) but entails a transit away from the imaginary, and toward the register of the symbolic. This is not only part of a psychotherapeutic practice, but a pedagogical act as well.

It is, thus, in the activity of those who intervene in the processes of subject formation—pedagogue and reformer—that their aggressiveness is laid bare.

The Subject in Higher Education: The Subject Supposed to Know

The very first "problem" the text addresses is related to the subject who teaches, and is enunciated as a problem of "faculty quality". The image it installs as critical to the quality of higher education is that of "well qualified and highly motivated faculty" (p. 23). By framing the notion of the subject who teaches around a concern for "the level of knowledge imparted to students", and their use of diverse methods, the discourse of the World Bank rests on a notion that relates to what Lacan termed the "subject supposed to know". Though developed in relation to a discussion about the analyst, as we will see, the concept bears important implications for an understanding of the role of the teacher, and consequently, their process of formation.

For Lacan, an indispensable element for transference to take place between analysand and analyst (and by extension, between student and teacher) is that the analysand/student must suppose that the analyst/teacher knows something he or she does not. In other words, it is an attribution of knowledge to a subject. This definition, Evans (1996) notes, "*emphasizes that it is the analysand's supposition of a subject who knows that initiates the analytic* [and pedagogical] *process, rather than the knowledge actually possessed by the analyst*" (p. 223).

The discourse of the World Bank, in its reiterative accent on knowledge possession as something factual and deliverable, suggest their belief in teachers as someone who actually knows. Someone who possesses a knowledge that is verifiable, preexistent and independent of the context where it is produced and disseminated. A strikingly similar notion appears in the documentation of Tuning, where in an intertextual discursive relation of support with the World Bank, it predefines 25 specific competencies that education programs should develop in their graduates (Reference Points for the Design and Delivery of Degree Programmes in Education—Tuning, 2009).

Rational as it may seem, at first sight, the installation of an image of faculty as those who actually know is problematic from several perspectives, but particularly from a psychoanalytic understanding of the intimate dynamics that take place in the pedagogical student–teacher relationship. Evans (1996) explains that in this particular relationship to knowledge, the analyst/teacher must be aware of the split between him and the knowledge that is attributed to him. Particularly, *"the analyst* [or teacher] *must realise that he only occupies the position of one who is presumed (by the analysand) to know, without fooling himself that he really does possess the knowledge attributed to him"*. He points out, citing Lacan, that *"the analyst must realize that, of the knowledge attributed to him by the analysand, he knows nothing"* (Lacan 1967, in Evans, p. 224).

One of the direct implications of this attribution is that the moment the analyst/teacher falls from the position of the subject supposed to know, and becomes one who simply knows a particular set of things, the analytical/pedagogical relationship disintegrates. In this sense, the imaginary construction of the World Bank and Tuning of the figure of those who teach as those who know is not one without plausible consequences for the ethos of the practice of education.

The Subject in Higher Education: The Educated Subject

It is not surprising that, both in the World Bank and Tuning, the subject is defined in relation to knowledge. But such definition is framed within a very particular type of knowledge. Apart from the very specific competencies defined by Tuning for each discipline,[2] the discourse of the

---

[2]For Education, the 25 specific competencies are mostly related to abilities for management and implementation of educational trends.

World Bank attempts a broader conceptualization, advocating for general education to be present in all institutions of higher education. Through this general education, the subject they hope to graduate is one who "*can think and write clearly, effectively and critically; has broad knowledge of other cultures; has some understanding and experience in thinking systematically about moral and ethical problems; has achieved depth in some field of knowledge*" (p. 84). Additionally, the educated person, it asserts, should have an informed acquaintance with the mathematical and experimental methods of the sciences, and with the main forms of the quantitative techniques "*needed to investigate the development of a modern society*" (p. 84).

This definition prioritizes a focus on cognitive skills, a type of knowledge delimited to cognition and numerical thinking. This prioritizing is also apparent in its framing of non-scientific knowledge (humanities) as a problematic element in their assessment of the current situation of higher education in relation to the economy. For the World Bank, "*Cultural traditions and infrastructure limitations also frequently cause students to study subjects, such as humanities and the arts, that offer limited job opportunities and lead to "educated unemployment". At the same time, there is often unmet demand for qualified science graduates*" (p. 24).

What is this attachment to objective, measurable knowledge signaling? What might be the symptom expressed in such strong adherence and imposition of rational, practical, observable and measurable knowledge?

On the one hand, rationalization—psychoanalysis has shown—is a defense mechanism. As Freud demonstrated, defenses are the way the ego reacts to fend off situations (from both the unconscious and the outside world) that might pose a threat to what is perceived as equilibrium, comfortable and known. As an anxious reaction, rationalization can be a form of the mechanism known as "reaction formation" (or the acting in the opposite direction of the desires felt) or a form of intellectualization typical in the neurotic.

On the other hand, the idealization of this kind of knowledge and its institutionalization signals an attitude with psychic consequences. As Deborah Britzman (2003) explains, "*...the belief in knowledge, at the level of the institution, often takes the form of idealization and systematicity: discussions of knowledge actually signal a loss of faith when they are arranged tightly in the actions of taxonomies, behavioural objectives, measurable outcomes, and instructional goals. In this design, thoughts do not await thinkers, and knowledge is only knowledge of actions*" (p. 124).

One of the consequences of such loss of faith is that the process of formation is reduced to the cognitive operations of thinking, expunging inner life and emotion. As Peter Taubman notes, the current practices in education, such as relentless testing in an age of accountability, "have replaced self-exploration, following one's interests, and journeys through madness" (2011, p. 157).

In the foreclosure of the acts of symbolization, interpretation, and persuasion (which are mediated by the movements of inner life and emotion) we witness the "breakdown of knowledge, the shattering of belief, the fracturing of emotional ties, and not learning" (Britzman 2003, p. 124). The specular image of education that appears in the discourse of the World Bank is full of significations but devoid of affection. But as psychoanalytic experience shows, the forgotten affective elements that are discarded or pushed to the sidelines do not disappear. As Britzman would note, these contents threaten to return, irrupt and ruin the aseptic arrangements of the institution.

Policy, the Super Ego, and the Phallus

As a discursive genre, the text "Peril and Promise" of the World Bank defines educational public policy today. Using rhetorical devices such as assertion, reiteration, rhetorical questions, rationalization, the use of utterance modalities of epistemic and deontic nature (cognitive-logical operations, and the expression of obligation and command) the discursive intention and effect is not that of offering suggestions to consider: it sets instructions to be followed by governments. As such, it is invested with power.

It must be noted here that the power it exerts is not just rhetorical, but it is backed and enacted through legal and economic regulations that dictate change at the level of language, practices and institutional conditions for education. The discourse of the World Bank, and its practical ramifications such as Tuning, dictate the law under which most educational activity now finds its logics to think, speak and act.

But how is it that this discourse arouses such wide acceptance and adherence to its mandate?; How is it that their conceptualization of education has penetrated the praxis of the discipline so deeply that their notions are now part of its common sense?; More importantly, how does it do it to be perceived not as an imposition of power but as an expression of (valid) authority?

I believe there are at least three closely related aspects that, in interrelation, help shed light on the psychic origin and effects of the discourse of the World Bank.

One of those aspects is the dynamics that take place in group psychology or the experience of a "collective mind". In his "Group Psychology and the Analysis of the Ego", Sigmund Freud (1949) explains the perspective of group psychology as a concern for the individual as a member of a collective, i.e. a profession, a guild, or an institution. In such a context, as is the case of the collective of teachers and other education professionals who work within institutional communities, we find the expression of a particular kind of instinct: that of the "group mind". Within that setting, Freud notes, individuals "feel, think and act in a manner quite different from that in which each individual would in a state of isolation" (p. 7). By bringing attention to the fact that our conscious acts are predicated on an unconscious substratum, he describes a series of phenomena that are proper to the collective mind, among which two are of interest for the context of our discussion.

One is that in a group "the sentiment of responsibility which always controls individuals disappears entirely" (p. 9), setting the stage for a felt need to accept the will of a leader, someone who carries the responsibility of vision, passion, and sense of direction.

The other phenomenon—classed among the hypnotic order—is that of contagion. "In a group", Freud explains, "every sentiment and act is contagious, and contagious to such degree that an individual readily sacrifices his personal interest to the collective interest" (p. 10).

Commenting on the forces of susceptibility and influence in the group psychology of education, Deborah Britzman (2003) points to a crucial aspect for our understanding of the guild's acceptance of curricular policy as authority. In the experiences of group membership, she suggests, "individuals appear to give up the more obdurate parts of their individuality for the sake of being loved…". (p. 111).

This search for love brings in the second interrelated aspect, that of the existence and effects of libidinal ties. These ties do not just animate the drive to know or sustain the relation of transference between student and teacher. They also create and maintain a sense of membership and belonging to a group. At the same time, Britzman notes, it is this substrate of emotion that creates a sense of identification with the leader (s) of the group and the libidinal ties to the authority.

But a third element that brings together the workings of group mentality and the libidinality of the adherence to authority can be found in the symbolic function of the phallus.

As a function, it starts early in the Oedipal drama, when the child associates the absence of the mother with the presence of the father (when she's not with me, it's because she's with him). The father then first appears as a rival phallic object and then as the one who is presumed to have the phallus, or the object of desire of the mother (Dor 1997). In this drama, the child needs to master this profound sense of loss by symbolizing the understanding that "he is not the one and only object of his mother's desire, that is, *the object that fills the lack in the Other (the phallus)*" (Dor 1997, p. 113). Once the child enters the realm of language (operates from the register of the symbolic) he achieves a symbolic mastery of the lost object. In an act mediated by repression, language structures a process of metaphorization, of signifying substitution, where the repression of the "phallic signifier, the signifier of the mother's desire" (Dor, p. 113) finds expression in a complete different signifier that takes its place. We can see here the dynamic of the enigmatic signifier in operation.

In what continues to operate throughout our lives in the ambivalence of desire between being like the other and having the other, the repressed phallic signifier appears in our (unconscious) desire to dictate the law (as a paternal metaphor of that who has the phallus) or comply with the law, and so gain the affection of the mother.

As Britzman (2003) notes, an important aspect of the phallus, for the context of our discussion, is that it inaugurates and sustains a simultaneous relationship between love and authority, which at first are experienced as the same.

To begin to understand the position of the World Bank's Task Force as policymakers (those who dictate the law), it helps to consider the fact that, in order to substitute for the object of desire lost in the primal oedipal drama, we turn to engaging our desire in the realm of objects through language. In order to accomplish this substitution, Dor explains, "desire must become speech in the form of a *demand*" (p. 118).

Is the expression of a demand through the language of policy a demand for love and attention?

In the symbolic substitution of desire for signifiers, desire "remains forever unsatisfied because it had to become language", Dor explains, and in becoming a demand, "desire gets more and more lost in the signifying chain of discourse", moving "from object to object, always referring to an indefinite series of substitutes and at the same time to an indefinite series of signifiers that symbolize these substitute objects" (p. 118).

As an expression of libidinal desire, curriculum shows throughout its history a reflection of such substitutive chain of phallic origin in its ongoing and continued demand for something else. For example, in the sixteenth century in colonial Spanish America, the curriculum demanded from teachers and students a focus on reading, writing and "virtuous good manners". During the seventeenth and eighteenth centuries prayer, grammar, math, and catechism were added to the official curriculum. From the nineteenth century and on the list of demands grows exponentially, to the present time where international agencies demand of education to be a regulator of the economy and the market.

The discourse of curricular policy (as a metaphor of the paternal law) exerts important psychic consequences on those who receive it and consume it. In providing the mirror image after which educators must conform to, the discourse produces two simultaneous effects. It intervenes in the construction of the ego of educators, providing the terms through which the ego will continue its job of reality testing and adaptation, creating the sediment of what is perceived as identity. At the same time, I would suggest that the discourse of curricular policy acts as the super-ego of the teaching profession. Drawing from the libidinal ties and group psychology of the professions, it positions itself as an authority figure. By doing that, just as in the Freudian account of the workings of the superego in relation to the ego, it builds on the residual traces of the parental authority figures to dictate the law, set limits, bring new needs to the fore, prioritize moral positions, and castigate the ego with feelings of guilt when—in alliance with the Id— it fails to comply with the demands set upon it or simply disregards them to allow the satisfaction of the instinctual desires from the drives. This positioning of the policy as super-ego and its effect at the level of the ego help explain, in part, the attitude of compliance among some teachers who feel they earn the moral reward of thinking of themselves as "good teachers" and "professionals" based on their ability to follow the protocols, standards, contents, and techniques dictated by the policy.

The Bottom Line:
Neurosenbildung and the Completion of the Symptom

The World Bank asserts its position of authority symbolically in its lexical selection, as it refers to the list of tasks they define for governments as "the bottom line".

At this point, to conclude, we can offer a general critical commentary of the symptomatic formations in its discourse and the psychic consequences they elicit.

The Imaginary and the Ethical

The international policy for higher education, which impacts teacher education in particular ways in terms of the transference, appears as a curricular discourse with strong manifestations at the level of the imaginary both in its origin and the register at which it is directed. This is evident primarily in the text's purpose of presenting specular images after which institutions, pedagogical practices, and individuals should resemble.

Remaining exclusively within the register of the imaginary, in the discourse, there is a complete absence of spaces of possibilities (or even regard) for expression from the register of the real (instincts, drives, memories), let alone their appearance in subjectivity through the register of the symbolic. As such, the conditions set do not promote significant space for the assertion of the subject in their own terms in the symbolization of their being, time and acts. From a Lacanian perspective, moving away from the imaginary and into the symbolic (through the real) is an essential condition for the reconstruction of subjectivity. In this sense, the curricular discourse promoted by the policy of the economic group is alienating. When there is no space for being, the only alternatives are to have and to act.

At the same time, in demanding the standardization and evaluation of professional formation according to the logics of a framework of economic productivity, the World Bank's Task Force attempts to define the contours, limits, and content of a definitive and authoritative ethics of education. In an anxious effort to make pedagogical and academic dynamics knowable, transparent, intelligible, and so controllable, they take it as the main objective to set guidelines and principles for the operation and assessment of higher education. "These benchmarks", they indicate, such as a competency-based curriculum, or the use of technologies, "offer guidance...helping to cut through the often confusing thicket of institutions and practices" (p. 91).

In an act propelled by aggressiveness, their discourse imposes meaning, a definition of what it means to teach, learn and work, making these acts transparent and known.[3] It ties its pedagogical formula to an ethical imperative, as the reasonable thing to do in the face of poverty and ever-growing economic challenges. Their approach then appears as the only sensible way to escape what is presented as an otherwise looming fate: being left behind the movement of progress. The closing remarks of the text put it in dramatic terms: implementing these reforms is urgent since we are in a "race between education and catastrophe" (p. 97).

Conceiving ethics as an a priori set of principles for a discipline, its practice, and its purpose is problematic. As Peter Taubman (2010) warns, such an approach to ethics is the same one that leads to terrorism, as it "imposes on everyone the particularities of a few" (p. 197).

Temporality, Neurosis and the Completion of the Unfinished Symptoms

As a discipline akin to psychoanalysis, education—Deborah Britzman (2009) points out—is "interminable because it is always incomplete and because it animates our own incompleteness" (p. 3). Acknowledging the momentariness of the pedagogical and the timelessness of its temporality involves also accepting the incalculability of its effects. Freud embraced this openness in the context of psychotherapy, asserting that "the outcome of...analysis is a matter of indifference", as long as "the compass of the ego has been extended" (1949, p. 73).

The notion of temporality in the discourse of the World Bank stands in stark contrast with the psychoanalytic understanding of education as ongoing and interminable. It operates in the definition of "new" realities and the urge to "waste no time" to escape a future marked by catastrophe. The new reality it describes as a present is marked by problems such as faculty who are "underqualified and lack motivation", students being "poorly taught", "underdeveloped curriculum" (p. 10), where the challenge of higher education is to "select, absorb and create new knowledge

---

[3] In contrast, for Lacan, the first virtue of knowledge is the capacity to face that which is not evident (Seminar IV).

more efficiently and rapidly" (p. 17). It's a present where "systematic knowledge has replaced experience" (p. 17).

The disavowal of experience (something built through biographical involvement in an interplay of past and present) and the insistence on the use-value of education as preparation for possible economic scenarios that do not yet exist reveal its orientation to the future.

In an open letter to right-wing Chilean politicians, the acclaimed queer novelist, activist, and performer Pedro Lemebel brings attention to this orientation toward the future as a common trait among the neoliberal. Referring to their participation in the overthrowing of socialist president Salvador Allende in the 70s, he writes: "*...we have not forgotten, and we will never forget, even if you hate it that the past will resurface when you least expect it. The past is inconvenient for you and all of your friends within the pact, that is why you all look cross-eyed and amnesic towards the future*". The World Bank's erasure and disavowal of experience and historicity do not mean the past will not come back. As psychoanalytic experience has shown, one forgets what one does not want to remember, but forgetting does not mean getting rid of.

If education shares with analysis in the status of being impossible and interminable, the teacher can be seen as akin to the analyst in the description of the nature of their practice and process of formation, as described by Freud and Lacan. As it becomes clear in pieces such as the Outline of Psychoanalysis (Freud 1949) and The Formation of the Analyst (Lacan, Écrits), the process of learning the discipline of the analyst/teacher is based on practical experience and sustained in academic knowledge (a firm base on linguistics and literature come to the fore in Lacan). But above all, one is formed in the transference, in the open and genuine conversation with the other, marked by the free flow of libidinal energy. Perhaps a difference in the education of the analyst and the teacher, as Deborah Britzman pointed out in a conversation, lies in that the education of the analyst accepts madness. At the same time, the education of teachers has also expelled and disavowed the Eros that animates its very practice.

The curricular policy outlined in Peril and Promise does away with anything that does not conform to what can be measured in its use value in the arena of labor market and economic exchange (recall here their deeming of the study of humanities and arts as a choice based on traditions and absence of better facilities, and as a cause of "educated unemployment"). Prioritizing efficiency and rapidness in the delivery and absorption of knowledge (thus their advocacy for the use of "innovative" methods and technology), it revamps a banking notion of education as a transaction. Within an ethics that frames education as a means to an economy of competition (hence the threat of being left behind), collaboration is rendered instrumental, and the attention to personal interests, talents, and the more intimate movements of inner life are absent from the conversation, relegated as irrelevant or useless for the new objectives of higher education.

Installing an imaginary construction of a professional based solely on cognitive terms, devoid of spaces for expression of the drives (the real) and the assertion of the subject (through the symbolic), the prescription of policy by the World Bank is a recipe for the triggering of various defense mechanisms. Particularly affecting the formation of teachers, the forcing of a process of certification that prioritizes actions, methods, the use of accessories (such as technologies) and a transactional attitude basically oriented to obtaining certain results from students, not only disavows the libidinal force that animates the pedagogical practice, together with the educator's dreams, aggressiveness, desires, memories, interests, wishes and fears that determine their understanding of their role and practice. In triggering defense mechanisms, such as rationalization, or the compulsion to comply with the (phallic) norm, they numb the teacher's attentiveness to the fragile emergence of moments and situations pregnant with the potential of educational significance.

But it does more. The conditions prescribed by the World Bank also set the stage for neuroses.

At a surface level, the symptomatology of mental-health among teachers has been reported as a growing concern in the last decade. An example of this is the BBC news report (26 March 2016) indicating that one in ten teachers have been prescribed anti-depressant drugs, while 79% of those polled reported anxiety and 86% sleeplessness. But the psychic disturbances that these symptoms are signaling do not only occur in the work setting, and take place much earlier, in the process of becoming a teacher.

In this process of becoming, of acquiring new substance (as van Humboldt would put it), or exercising the vocation of being more, and acquiring "more humanity" (Savater 2004), teachers are bound to experience anxiety, and the exposure to new and challenging discourses soon trigger the ego's defense mechanisms to mediate between the maintenance of what is familiar and the need to change. In this context, as

Deborah Britzman (2003) suggests, "the smallest detail or the tiniest word can provoke the ego's defenses" (p. 87).

In this context, the experience of anxiety, and other psychic disturbances that on occasion find somatic expression are not always something to be avoided or "cured". As central to the processes of transformation, they are inevitable and—arguably—necessary for the configuration of subjectivity in individuality.

The conditions outlined by the World Bank, however, elicit a different form of symptomatic response. Defining education mainly on terms of cognition, the measurable, and expunging what makes subjective (re)construction possible—that which makes the hearts of teachers beat and break (Britzman 2003)—the formation of teachers is rendered a *neurosenbildung*: an education that—built on imaginary constructions of an ego ideal—leaves the subject in the ongoing and anxious attempt to resemble the ideal image set as expectation, with the subsequent sense of failure and guilt, and eventual renunciation of responsibility that the group mentality allows, when falling short of what is set as standard.

Within the terms of the World Bank, curriculum is treated as a "fixed body, totalized and transparent to itself, rather than as a living, contingent and resymbolizable response to our desires, fears, and dreams", Peter Taubman maintains, having as a direct implication that both teachers' and students' subjectivity is excised (2011, p. 172). Under such conditions, it is no surprise that the result would be a *neurosenbildung*, a notion first used by Anna Freud, characterized by a chain of psychic dynamics, where there is "an arousal of danger, and anxiety, a defense, a compromise formation, and finally a symptom" (Britzman 2003, p. 87). Symptoms, in this case, being expressions of neuroses.

A neurosis is, for Lacan, a resulting symptom constituted by the operations of repression—in this case, the repression of components of subjectivity such as those mentioned by Taubman. But Sigmund Freud's description of the mental life of the neurotic allows for a consideration of the political implications in relation to policy. A state of neurosis, he writes, is characterized by a "sense of guilt or consciousness of guilt, even though the patient does not feel it and is not aware of it" and adds that "it is a portion of resistance" contributed by a superego peculiarly severe and cruel" (1949, p. 75). In this sense, thinking of educational policy as taking the role of the teaching profession's superego helps understand, in part, the growing numbers of mental health issues among educators, but also their symptomatic demand for norms, protocols, concern about expectations, and the overall orientation to how things "should be done".

Freud points out that this neurotic form of resistance" "does not interfere with our intellectual work, but it makes it ineffective", and in what sounds very much in line with Foucault's view of critical work as the art of not being governed so much, Freud suggests how to proceed: we need to "attempt the gradual demolition of the hostile superego" (p. 75).

References

Bracher, M. (1993). *Lacan, Discourse and Social Change: A Psychoanalytic Cultural Criticism*. Ithaca and London: Cornell University Press.
Britzman, D. (2003). *After-Education: Anna Freud, Melanie Klein, and Psychoanalytic Histories of Learning*. New York: SUNY Press.
Britzman, D. (2009). *The Very Thought of Education: Psychoanalysis and the Impossible Professions*. Albany: SUNY Press.
Britzman, D. (2010). *Freud and Education*. New York: Routledge.
Dor, J. (1997). *Introduction to the Reading of Lacan: The Unconscious Structured Like a Language*. New York: Rowman & Littlefield.
Evans, D. (1996). *An Introductory Dictionary of Lacanian Psychoanalysis*. New York: Routledge.
Freud, S. (1949). *An Outline of Psychoanalysis*. New York: W. W. Norton.
Gonzáles, J., & Wagenaar, R. (Eds.). (2008). *Universities' Contribution to the Bologna Process, an Introduction*. Tuning Project. Spain: Publicaciones de la Universidad de Deusto.
Pinar, W. (1975). *Curriculum Theorizing: The Reconceptualists*. Berkeley: McCutchan Pub. Corp.
Savater, F. (2004). *El Valor de Educar*. Barcelona: Ariel.
Taubman, P. (2010). Alan Badiou, Jacques Lacan and the Ethics of Teaching. *Educational Philosophy and Theory, 42*(2), 196–212.
Taubman, P. (2011). *Disavowed Knowledge: Psychoanalysis, Education and Teaching*. New York: Routledge.
The World Bank. (2000). *Higher Education in Developing Countries: Peril and Promise*.

CHAPTER 5

Concluding Thoughts

Abstract This concluding chapter recapitulates the three points we set out to achieve throughout this book and offers some afterthoughts on what they might imply for an understanding of curriculum. First, the theorizing we performed revealed curriculum in its nature and function as a symptom. It revealed that what is at stake in educational experience is the assertion and constitution of ourselves as subjects. Second, our approach to criticism appeared as the ability to recognize the truth of the symptom as they appear, emphasizing attunement and attentiveness to the phenomena we encounter. Finally, our critique disclosed that the implications of the global policy of curricular reform are more decisive at a subjective level of those affected by it, rather than a mere issue of methods.

Keywords Curriculum theory · Educational policy · Educational research · Psychoanalysis

The categories and the analysis presented thus far show that rather than reaching a conclusion as a closure or end point of a discussion, they represent potential starting points for new ways of reading, analyzing, and understanding educational phenomena. In this concluding section, then, instead of forcing a final word on the matter, we will recapitulate some of the points we set out to achieve at the beginning and offer some afterthoughts on what they might imply for an understanding of curriculum.

In the first section of this book, our intent was to gain an understanding of curriculum that would take into account the more inward aspects of psychic dynamics that operate in decisive ways in the formation of the subject. The theorizing we performed drawing on curricular theory and psychoanalysis revealed curriculum in its nature and function as a symptom. But before we can refer to some of the implications that such a theory of curriculum entails, we must first dispel a basic misconception that has taken root in education regarding the notion of theory. It is not uncommon to encounter among educationalists today a demand for theory to be practical. Such sentiment is patently present in the expectation for a theoretical account to tell us "How will this help me in my work next Monday?". This expectation and demand for theory to "do" things are, as we have shown, a symptomatic expression of a certain anxiety about being in the world. A world that is experienced as frightening in its complexity and unpredictability, that might expose our fragility, and that opens up the possibility of having to face the unknown existential aspects of our human condition, is met with a compulsion to act, to intervene, to prescribe how things should be done rather than describe them as they are.

Theory, in its ancient Greek root (θεωρία) means to contemplate. To theorize, then, is an act of "beholding" a phenomenon, of contemplating it in a way that brings about an speculative understanding of it. In the context of this discussion, theorizing means engaging with the language of the field, criticising it, determining the intellectual history of the vocabulary it uses, conceptualizing its practices, and envisioning different ways to think and talk about the phenomena it encounters. As such, the aspects of curriculum we have developed across this book delineate the contours of a particularly *Lacanian* theory of curriculum, one that has brought about an understanding of it as a symptom, and a set of descriptions of its functions that work as categories for its critique.

The notion of symptom disclosed to us an aspect of curriculum as an expression of the existential drama of being and becoming. It revealed that what is at stake in educational experience is the assertion and constitution of ourselves as subjects, and along with it, the possibility of being undone and shattered by it at the same time. In this sense, the unfinished symptom in curriculum appears a placeholder for what might happen in one's own process of formation, a process that is, for the most part, open to risk and failure. It is fraught with anxiety and fear, but also hope and love. The unfinished symptom is a placeholder for what desire produces:

a tension between what was, what could have been, and what might be: the fear of missing and losing, but also the drive to go after the not-yet.

As we came to realize, the symptomatic nature of curriculum is closely related to an issue of knowledge. In its appearance, the symptom articulates a truth, and as Lacan emphasized, symptoms *are* truth. This truth is not the kind of truth one might commonly associate with propositional knowledge (knowing *about* something, facts, information), but is rather a more profound sense of what is actually the case about ourselves at a more intimate level. Although academic knowledge does play a fundamental role in the formation of subjectivity (and is in itself a product of desire), the truth of the symptom is what gives us a sense of the Real.

Lacan insisted that, since symptoms are articulated in the signifying order, they can only be interpreted within that order, that is, in the domain of language and words. This is the basic premise on which our approach to curricular criticism—the second task we set out to achieve—finds its foundation. Understanding curriculum as symptom, then, invites us to reread the phenomena of education. This implies reading not just "between the lines" but actually reading the lines themselves again. It is in this phenomenological stance that we can be attuned to the reality of the phenomena that we encounter and that gives itself to us in its very mode of appearance. Reading and interpreting the symptoms articulated in curriculum and its language can perhaps be compared to a story about a wheelbarrow as told by Zlavoj Zizek in a commentary for *The Guardian* (19 February 2005):

> Recall the old story about a worker suspected of stealing. Every evening, when he was leaving the factory, the wheelbarrow he was rolling in front of him was carefully inspected, but it was always empty - till, finally, the guards got the point: what the worker was stealing were the wheel-barrows themselves.

An approach to criticism that is able to recognize the truth of the symptom as they appear, in the "wheelbarrows" themselves, emphasizes a stance of attunement and attentiveness to the phenomena we encounter. Rather than a free-floating, whimsical interpretation—as a positivist might claim—the phenomenological attitude of a Lacanian approach to criticism requires instead to be fully grounded in and with the world. As such, it is a rejection of the nihilism that hides behind the devotion to facts, the useful, the measurable, and the effective, and invites us instead to engage with ourselves and with the other in a hermeneutic stance: to regain a sense of awe and respect for the phenomenon as it offers itself to us, to describe it in the authenticity of its singularity, and to discern the substantial and universal aspects that compose it. It entails, in sum, a relation of love. Perfect love casts out the fear that drives the empiricist attitude and the compulsion to act.

In its Greek root, the word "truth"—*aletheia*—holds special significance for our discussion. With the prefix *a-* "not" and *lethe* "oblivion" or "forgetfulness", truth is that which should not be forgotten. Truth remains truth, even in spite of disavowal, repression, or sublimation. And this is perhaps the importance of the symptom: it is the return of truth.

In the third part of this book, the intent was to demonstrate the methodological approach to curricular criticism using the analytical categories developed throughout the previous two sections. To do that, I used as an object of analysis the text *Peril and Promise*, the World Bank's blueprint for global curricular reform. Reading it as a signifying chain that articulates symptomatic expression, our mode of critique disclosed to us that, technical as it may sound, the implications of the policy are more decisive at a subjective level of those affected by it, rather than a mere issue of methods, protocols, and applications.

Considering that changing the language and terms of an activity changes its sense, practice, and those who are attracted to it—as the policy of the World Bank has contributed to in higher education—makes one consider that perhaps forcing the process of teacher formation to comply with the standards and demands of other professions has been psychically detrimental to the experience and role of being an educator. One cannot help but wonder what would happen if priests or artists were submitted to the same standards, expectations, and evaluations of an ever more homogenized and product-driven, fact-based professional certification. While the consideration of the evidence of the state of the matter would point to the suggestion of emancipating teacher education from the professional arena as a sensible though controversial solution, we still need to grapple with the state of psychic dynamics as they are presently conditioned.

The unfinished symptoms prompted by the conditions laid out by the international educational policy can only find completion with the participation of a subject that accepts the terms of that interpellation. Such response is what we find in the triggering of neuroses. In Lacanian terms, the desire of the neurotic is the demand of the Other. This is what operates in those wanting a law, a norm, a regulation, a method prescribed by the Other. But historically, teachers have also demonstrated resilience, and a capacity to assert themselves as subjectively existing actors.

The setting of curricular conditions is a political arrangement, and the political is essentially a symbolic act. The discourse of policy, then, finds strength in that in its narrative it takes up the function of enunciation and symbolic mediation. It is in discourse—at the register of the symbolic—that unconscious material finds expression, in the linguistic terms in which the unconscious is structured: association, substitution, metonymy, and metaphor. In the free exercise of symbolic representation, we find the more authentic and profound expression of what makes our subjectivity—and its ongoing process of reconstruction—not only possible but actually filled with a sense of the sublime.

Standardization, on the other hand, by taking away the symbolic function in the other, strips the subject from its capacity to sense and attune to the sublime, turning that subject transparent, knowable, and ultimately—in the world of labor—replaceable.

In reading and engaging with text, Lacan points out, "People don't understand anything, that is perfectly true, for a while, but the writings do something to them" (2013, p. 70). In the third section of this book, I attempted to show the psychical dynamics at play in the initiation of that which curricular policy text does to people. Yet, since it is only an initiation, an unfinished symptom, one cannot predict in what ways policies will affect us. It is particularly in a context such as this, and in spite of its conditions, where Lacan's reminder that we are always responsible for our position as subjects is timely. In our work in higher education, it is an act of love to engage in the ongoing critical activity of untying and severing of the knots of imaginary servitude that the policies of standardization impose.

Reference

Lacan, J. (2013). *The Triumph of Religion, Preceded by Discourse to Catholics.* Cambridge: Polity Press.

Index

A
act, 2, 13, 16, 17, 20–24, 27–29, 34, 35, 37–40, 43, 45, 48, 50, 51, 55, 58, 62, 67–69, 72–74
alterity, 3
analyzing, 1, 45, 61, 83
anxiety, 2, 16, 19, 24–29, 46, 50, 79, 80, 84
appearance, 2, 5, 6, 10, 16, 47–49, 54, 76, 85

B
becoming, 2, 4, 7, 11, 12, 17, 25, 28, 48, 62, 75, 79, 84
being, 2, 3, 5, 9, 11, 12, 14, 17, 21–26, 37, 48, 50, 51, 53, 56, 63, 65, 67, 73, 74, 76, 84, 86
Bernfeld, Siegfried, 5, 6
Bildung, 3, 4, 11
Bobbitt, Franklin, 10
Britzman, Deborah, 13, 15, 16, 19, 20, 22–28, 34, 35, 42, 43, 46, 48, 50, 56, 62, 64, 71–74, 77, 78, 80

C
clinical, 4, 20, 25
compulsion, 17, 40, 51, 79, 84, 86
conversation, 26, 30, 31, 43, 46, 78, 79
critical pedagogy, 16, 18
criticism, 34–36, 44, 45, 47, 55, 58, 62, 66, 85, 86
critique, 6, 8, 33–39, 41–43, 45, 46, 49, 50, 54–56, 58, 63, 84, 86
cultivation, 2, 3, 10, 11
cultural, 3, 7, 9, 13, 14, 16, 36, 44, 54, 55, 57, 71
curriculum studies, 2, 3, 7, 10, 12, 34, 35, 39, 42, 57

D
defense mechanisms, 16, 27, 79
desire, 2, 5–7, 14, 16, 17, 19, 21–24, 26, 28, 30, 31, 34, 36, 40, 43, 45, 46, 49, 51, 53, 63, 71, 74
discourse, 5, 6, 10, 14, 15, 17, 18, 22, 26, 28, 34, 35, 40, 42–45, 48,

50, 54, 55, 57, 58, 62–66, 69, 70, 72, 73, 75
drama, 2, 7, 8, 25, 49, 74, 84
dreams, 17, 57, 79, 80
drives, 5, 6, 11, 21, 30, 45, 53, 75, 76, 79, 86
dynamics, 6, 7, 13, 15, 20, 21, 34, 35, 42, 46, 62–64, 70, 73, 76, 80, 84, 86, 87

E
Educating, 1–3
education, 1–3, 6, 10–13, 15, 16, 18, 20, 22, 23, 25–27, 29, 30, 33–35, 40, 41, 43, 47, 49, 50, 55–58, 61–73, 75–78
educators, 2, 17, 28, 75, 80
Ego, 16, 21–23, 27–29, 67, 68
enjoyment, 2, 6, 7, 47
existence, 3, 7, 15, 17, 18, 36, 47, 54, 73

F
failure, 1, 15, 17, 18, 80, 84
formation, 2–4, 6, 9, 10, 13, 15, 21–25, 35, 46, 49, 51, 55, 62, 63, 65, 68, 69, 71, 72, 76, 78
Foucault, Michel, 37–39, 81
Freud, Sigmund, 1, 2, 4–7, 15, 16, 18, 20, 25–27, 34, 35, 42, 43, 45, 50, 56, 58, 61, 67, 71, 73, 77, 78

G
governing, 1, 37, 38

H
Huebner, Dwayne, 11, 30, 31, 45, 51

human, 3, 7, 10, 11, 15, 25, 36, 37, 44, 45, 49, 54, 56, 57, 84
humanities, 3, 4, 44, 71, 78

I
Imaginary, 7, 21–24, 29, 30, 34, 45, 49, 64, 67–70, 76, 79, 80, 87
impossible profession, 1, 2
individual, 3, 5, 6, 10, 30, 37
individuality, 22, 73, 80
instruction, 3
interpellation, 18, 47, 65, 67, 86
intuition, 2

J
jouissance, 6, 21, 45, 47, 53

K
knowledge, 3, 8, 13, 14, 20, 24, 28, 37–39, 44, 55, 56, 58, 63, 65, 66, 69–72, 77–79, 85

L
Lacan, Jacques, 2, 4–8, 12, 15, 19–29, 31, 34, 36, 42–49, 51–53, 55, 57, 58, 66, 68–70, 77, 78
Lacanian, 2, 4–8, 12, 13, 21, 30, 35, 42, 44, 63, 64, 76, 84–86
language, 4, 5, 7, 11–13, 15, 21–25, 28, 30, 31, 34, 41, 43, 44, 46, 48–53, 57, 58, 61, 62, 64, 68, 72
love, 8, 12, 43, 54, 55, 68, 73, 74, 84, 86, 87

M
method, 8, 33, 40–42
mirror stage, 12, 22, 48, 49

N
narcissistic, 16, 19, 67

O
the other, 7, 36, 54, 55, 74, 86, 87

P
philosophy, 3, 4, 11
Pinar, William, 3, 11, 12, 14, 19, 23, 34, 35, 39, 42, 43, 50, 54, 57, 62, 64
pleasure, 2, 21, 27
policy, 8, 56, 57, 64, 68, 72–76, 78–80, 86, 87
political, 9, 14, 16, 44, 45, 62–66, 68, 80, 87
politics, 3, 5, 16, 18, 19, 38
practice, 3, 4, 7, 11, 13, 14, 17, 18, 26, 29, 30, 34, 35, 38–40, 43, 49, 54, 56–58, 68–70, 77
psychic, 3–6, 13, 15, 17, 18, 21–23, 30, 35, 42–44, 61–63, 68, 71, 73, 75, 76
psychical, 15, 21, 25–27, 34, 36, 42, 67, 87
psychology, 3, 6, 24, 29, 30, 48–50, 57, 68, 69, 73, 75

R
Real, 7, 8, 21–23, 28, 30, 31, 34, 45, 50, 53, 56, 64, 76, 79, 85
reality, 2, 16, 23, 25, 28, 30, 53, 62, 68, 75, 77, 85
Reconceptualization, 3
reconstruction, 3, 12, 17, 18, 31, 39, 57, 58, 76, 87
registers, 21, 23, 64
repressed, 5, 25, 30, 74
resistance, 16, 18, 20, 27, 35, 45, 56, 80, 81
return, 2, 5, 7, 20, 25, 38, 46, 62, 64, 72, 86

S
schooling, 3, 6, 11, 12, 16, 34, 35, 62
self, 2, 3, 7, 12, 19, 21, 22, 27–30, 35, 37, 39, 40, 43, 47, 49, 56, 58, 67, 69, 72
signified, 4, 52, 57
signifier, 4–7, 12, 22, 24–26, 34, 51–55, 57, 58, 74
social, 3, 5, 6, 9, 11, 12, 16, 17, 19, 29, 36, 40, 44, 45, 57, 67, 68
standardization, 10, 27, 62, 63, 76, 87
students, 9, 17, 19, 22, 28–31, 66, 69, 75, 77, 79, 80
study, 3, 4, 7, 11, 12, 14, 15, 33, 35, 37, 41, 42, 45, 64, 78
subject, 2, 5, 9–13, 16, 17, 20–24, 26, 29, 31, 35, 39, 41–43, 46, 48, 49, 51–55, 57, 62–64, 69–71, 76
subjectivity, 2, 7, 11, 12, 14, 15, 17–19, 21, 35, 39, 44, 46–49, 53, 55–57, 63, 76, 80, 85, 87
suffering, 2, 6, 7, 16, 17, 19, 23–25, 27, 36, 52, 53, 68
Symbolic, 6, 7, 21–23, 50, 53, 64
symptomatic expression, 2, 49, 84, 86
symptoms, 2, 5, 7, 20, 24, 25, 28, 29, 34, 35, 42, 46, 47, 54, 57, 61, 63–65, 77, 79, 80

T
Taubman, Peter, 13, 17–20, 24, 26, 29, 30, 33, 40, 48–50, 56, 62, 72, 77, 80
teachers, 9, 17, 27–29, 31, 36, 40, 56, 62, 70, 73, 75, 78–80, 87

temporality, 34, 41, 49–51, 77
text, 8, 14, 35, 57, 58, 63–69, 72, 76, 77, 86, 87
theorization, 8, 26, 41
transference, 12, 13, 20, 21, 26, 29–31, 45, 46, 58, 61, 63, 69, 73
Tyler, Ralph, 10, 11

U
unconscious, 4, 5, 13, 15–25, 30, 35, 40, 43, 44, 46, 47, 51, 53–55, 57, 58, 61, 63, 71, 73

understanding, 2–4, 7, 11, 14, 16, 18, 22, 24, 26, 28, 29, 34, 35, 39, 40, 44, 46, 48–50, 53, 57, 58, 61, 63, 64, 66, 69–71

V
von Humboldt, Wilhelm, 3, 79

CPSIA information can be obtained
at www.ICGtesting.com
Printed in the USA
LVHW06*0910251018
PP14070700001B/1/P